Contours of Christian Philosophy
C. STEPHEN EVANS, *Series Editor*

Contours of Christian Philosophy
C. STEPHEN EVANS, *Series Editor*

Ethics

Approaching Moral Decisions

Arthur F. Holmes

InterVarsity Press
Downers Grove, Illinois, U.S.A.
Leicester, England

InterVarsity Press
P.O. Box 1400, Downers Grove, Illinois 60515, U.S.A.
38 De Montfort Street, Leicester LE1 7GP, England

InterVarsity Press, U.S.A., is the book-publishing division of Inter-Varsity Christian Fellowship, a student movement active on campus at hundreds of universities, colleges and schools of nursing. For information about local and regional activities, write IVCF, 233 Langdon St., Madison, WI 53703.

Inter-Varsity Press, England, is the publishing division of the Universities and Colleges Christian Fellowship (formerly the Inter-Varsity Fellowship), a student movement linking Christian Unions in universities and colleges throughout the British Isles, and a member movement of the International Fellowship of Evangelical Students. For information about local and national activities in Great Britain write to UCCF, 38 De Montfort Street, Leicester LE1 7GP.

All Scripture quotations, unless otherwise indicated, are from the Revised Standard Version of the Bible, copyrighted 1946, 1952, © 1971, 1973.

*ISBNs: USA 0-87784-342-2   USA 0-87784-339-2 (Contours of Christian Philosophy set)
        UK 0-85110-724-9*

Printed in the United States of America

British Library Cataloguing in Publication Data

Holmes, Arthur F.
    Ethics—(Contours of Christian philosophy)
    1. Christian ethics
    I. Title   II. Series
    241   BJ1251

    ISBN 0-85110-724-9

Library of Congress Cataloging in Publication Data

Holmes, Arthur Frank, 1924-
    Ethics, thinking about morality.

    (Contours of Christian philosophy)
    Includes bibliographic references.
    1. Ethics.   2. Christian ethics.   I. Title.   II. Series.
BJ1012.H65   1984   241   84-22770
ISBN 0-87784-342-2

---

18   17   16   15   14   13
98   97   96   95

GENERAL PREFACE

The Contours of Christian Philosophy series will consist of short introductory-level textbooks in the various fields of philosophy. These books will introduce readers to major problems and alternative ways of dealing with those problems. These books, however, will differ from most in that they will evaluate alternative viewpoints not only with regard to their general strength, but also with regard to their value in the construction of a Christian world and life view. Thus, the books will explore the implications of the various views for Christian theology as well as the implications that Christian convictions might have for the philosophical issues discussed. It is crucial that Christians attain a greater degree of philosophical awareness in order to improve the quality of general scholarship and evangelical theology. My hope is that this series will contribute to that end.

Although the books are intended as examples of Christian scholarship, it is hoped that they will be of value to others as well; these issues should concern all thoughtful persons. The assumption which underlies this hope is that complete neutrality in philosophy is neither possible nor desirable. Philosophical work always reflects a person's deepest commitments. Such commitments, however, do not preclude a genuine striving for critical honesty.

C. Stephen Evans
Series Editor

I
The Moral Revolution

*I*n the 1960s a moral revolution that had been brewing for decades burst upon us. Some of it was highly commendable, especially the refusal to accept abuses of political, economic and military power. But in rejecting establishment ways it also changed accepted sexual morality, it took individualism to narcissistic extremes, and it placed in jeopardy existing ideals for marriage and family, work and government. This in turn has produced conservative reactions that polarize us both morally and politically over issues like human rights, criminal punishment and legislating morality, as well as sex and war.

In this mixed-up environment the Christian has to pick a way. Again and again the old groupings of left and right no longer seem helpful. Sloganeering and dogmatizing settle nothing, nor do emotional tirades and protests really help us sort things through in a thoughtful, biblical fashion. If we are to find our way and play a constructive role in the dialog of our times, we need to

understand the theoretical foundations of current views and to
develop a Christian ethic that can be applied to current concerns.

An Introduction to Ethics

This book attempts to contribute to that end. It is a Christian introduction to ethics, to both ethical theory and moral application.
Ethics is about the good (that is, what values and virtues we
should cultivate) and about the right (that is, what our moral
duties may be). It examines alternative views of what is good and
right; it explores ways of gaining the moral knowledge we need;
it asks why we ought to do right; and it brings all this to bear on
the practical moral problems that arouse such thinking in the first
place.

Plainly this differs from the way other disciplines address moral
problems. Sociology and anthropology, as social and behavioral
sciences, describe human behaviors and the functioning of social
institutions, trying to explain them causally in the light of gen-
eralized theories about human and social behavior. For many
centuries these disciplines along with political science and economics were regarded as branches of philosophy, extensions of
ethical theory. But over the past century, in coming to function
as empirical sciences, their interest in moral problems has focused
increasingly on the *causes* of particular problems and on the social
consequences. While ethical discussion and moral action are deeply
indebted to them for this, ethics as such is interested less in what
people in fact do than in what they *ought* to do, less in what their
values presently are and more in what their values *ought* to be. In
that it addresses the truth of our moral beliefs, it is a "normative"
discipline.

Ethics is in many regards more closely related to religion than
to social science, and the Judeo-Christian tradition is one of the
main historical sources of the moral heritage of the West. Accordingly this chapter will ask what ethics contributes to Christian
thinking and, reciprocally, what Christianity contributes to eth-

ics. Chapters two through five examine some widespread views that appear unsympathetic to a Christian ethic, some of which deny that moral beliefs can be true at all, while others limit themselves to weighing the observable consequences of our actions. In chapters six through eight, I outline a proposed Christian ethic in dialog with other ethical approaches. This proposal is applied to four representative moral issues in chapters nine through twelve. The final chapter brings us back to the relation of religion to ethics as it discusses moral character rather than moral actions: not what we should do, but the kind of persons we should be.

The Bible and Ethics

All religions are concerned with the promulgation of certain values and the cultivation of specific virtues, and most religions try to transform aspects of moral behavior. Religion and morality are closely linked, and Christianity is no exception to this. It too identifies values to be propagated and virtues to be cultivated; and it too speaks to various kinds of behavior. Whether our point of reference is the Ten Commandments, the book of Proverbs, the Old Testament prophets, the Sermon on the Mount or the letters of Paul, whether it is the historic teachings of the church or contemporary statements by ecclesiastical bodies, both Protestant and Catholic, the connection is plain. Religion comes hand in hand with an ethic.

Yet this observation may make some believers uneasy, as if a conflict of interest exists. If I have a religious commitment, why do I need an ethic? If I practice love, what more can anyone want? And perhaps most of all, if my religion teaches morality, what else can philosophical ethics contribute? Isn't the Bible alone sufficient? Might not anything further muddy the waters? Might it not lead us away from true paths of righteous living?

Of course, one answer may well be that we need to see what biblical morality can *contribute* to ethics, not just what ethics contributes to biblical Christianity. Both questions in fact face us, but I want first to confront our original question head-on.

The Contribution of Ethics

What can biblical morality gain from philosophical ethics? One obvious response is that the Bible gives us a vast repertoire of ethical material in different literary forms and from different historical and cultural contexts. We have a succinct summary in the Ten Commandments, extended casuistry (case applications) in the Mosaic code, epigrammatic wisdom in Proverbs, reflections on life's meaning and values in Ecclesiastes, preaching of social justice in the prophets, down-to-earth homilies in the Gospels and systematic statements in Paul's letters. To gain the overall picture, not only on particular topics but on whatever all-embracing principles there may be, we must understand each part in relation to the whole. If then we want to apply biblical morality systematically to the problems of our day, we need to find within this immense potpourri some logical structure that will enable us to follow the biblical implications further than what is explicitly stated. The task of theological ethics lies in exhibiting the structures implicit in biblical thought, but in doing so theology inevitably learns from philosophical efforts at shaping an ethic.

Another response to the believer who questions the need for ethics is still more basic: Christians do not claim that the Bible is exhaustive, that it tells us everything we can know or can benefit ethically from knowing. It is silent about many things, including many moral problems we face today—problems in bio- and medical ethics, for example, problems about responsibility to unborn generations and about population control. Someone may say that we should draw our conclusions on such matters from other things the Bible says, perhaps from more general principles. But then we have invoked a structure of ethical thought which distinguishes general principles from more specific matters and which employs modes of moral reasoning. This is precisely what ethical theory is about.

Again, we are confronted at times with moral dilemmas in which every available option is morally undesirable and a decision cannot be avoided or postponed. Suppose that in Nazi-occupied Holland you are hiding Jews in your attic and the Gestapo comes searching for them. Do you lie to save innocent lives, or do you forfeit innocent lives to save lying? Whatever you do will violate some moral rule or another. How then do you choose, and to what extent are you blameworthy? Ethics addresses such questions about moral choices and exceptions to moral rules, and about the extent of moral responsibility.

Someone might respond that it is enough to love God with heart and soul and to love my neighbor as myself: then I can safely do as I want; I am free. But are love and liberty enough? Christian liberty is not the license to do as I want, but is rather being liberated to live within what God's law requires. And love alone does not tell me what I *ought* to want and to do in every kind of situation; it still needs (and surely wants) *instruction* in righteousness of the sort the Bible gives. If I need and want more explicit moral guidance than liberty and love alone provide, then I will use every resource which God provides.

Scripture, of course, is not God's only revelation of himself and his will. The first three chapters of Romans are quite explicit that, in addition to God's special revelation of his law to Israel, we are accountable for a general revelation in the creation itself, and the Christian can rightly regard philosophical ethics as an attempt to understand that general revelation. Of course, not all ethicists see their task that way, and this fact often distorts how they interpret moral matters. The Christian will therefore want his philosophical and biblical ethics to go hand in hand, the biblical informing the philosophical wherever possible, and the philosophical serving the biblical.

The Contribution of the Bible
What does the Bible contribute to philosophical ethics? I shall

develop some of these suggestions further in later chapters, but for the present we may note the following biblical input into ethics.

1. It gives a theological basis for our moral obligation, in terms of our obligation to do the will of God, the Creator and Lawgiver. (We shall return to this in chapter eight.)

2. It gives an account of the relation of morality to God's purposes in creation, our perversion of those purposes through sin and our restoration to righteous living by the grace of God. (This will guide chapters six and following.)

3. We learn the principles of justice and love which describe God's character and should also characterize us (chapters six and thirteen).

4. It reveals the moral law of God, declaring duties in many areas of human life. This is summarized in the Ten Commandments and spelled out by precept and example throughout Scripture. (See chapter seven.)

5. From love for God and gratitude for his mercies come the motivation and dynamic for moral living (chapter thirteen).

6. The Bible depicts the ideals and promise of the kingdom of God that Christ came to establish, first in our hearts and lives and eventually throughout the entire world. (See chapters six, nine and eleven, for example.)

What we can hope to gain is an ethical structure that draws the many aspects of biblical morality into a coherent whole and guides our thinking about moral issues in other than biblical times and cultures. We can learn to distinguish universal and unchanging principles that transcend cultural and historical differences from case applications in culturally variable situations. We can look for ways of addressing philosophical concerns in ethics and of entering into dialog with other approaches. And this in turn can contribute to apologetics an awareness of why and how a Christian ethic does and does not differ from its non-Christian counterparts, and wherein it can take us further.

2

Cultural Relativism

E thics, we have said, is not an empirical science concerned with explaining existing moral practices, but a normative discipline interested in the truth or falsity of moral beliefs. This difference sometimes leads to conflicting points of view. Compare, for instance, the ethicist's emphasis on true moral beliefs with the following statement by anthropologist William Sumner.

It is of the first importance to notice that, from the first acts by which men try to satisfy needs, each act stands by itself, and looks no further than the immediate satisfaction. From recurrent needs arise habits for the individual and customs for the group, but these results are consequences which were never conscious, and never foreseen or intended. . . . a higher stage of mental development must be reached, before they can be used as a basis from which to deduce rules for meeting, in the future, problems whose pressure can be foreseen. The folkways, therefore, are not creations of human purpose and wit. They are like products of natural forces which men unconsciously set in operation, . . . which are handed down by tradition and admit of no exception or variation, yet change to meet new conditions, still within the same limited methods, and without rational reflection or purpose.[1]

Notice two implications of this statement that challenge the ethicist's emphasis on moral truth. First, moral practices vary with and depend on human needs and social conditions. Second, moral attitudes and practices are basically noncognitive responses rather than the product of rational direction. These views are often extended beyond primitive folkways to modern cultures and their moral codes. This chapter examines the first view, namely, cultural relativism; the next chapter will look at the second view, the emotivist interpretation of ethics.

Cultural relativism is the view that moral beliefs and practices vary with and depend on the human needs and social conditions of particular cultures, so that no moral beliefs can be universally true. There can be no universal "oughts." We shall distinguish within this definition a "diversity thesis" and a "dependency thesis."

The Diversity Thesis

Moral practices and beliefs do in fact vary from culture to culture and at different times in history, and none are universal. While assuming this thesis is descriptively correct, just how relevant is it to the ethicist's questions about moral truth? Since the ethicist is talking about what people *ought* to do or believe, not what in fact they *do,* this thesis does not logically deny what the ethicist claims. *Descriptive* statements do not necessarily contradict *normative* ones and so do not themselves settle the issue. But is it at least telling if all moral practices do indeed vary from culture to culture?

Let us look more closely. Are *all* moral practices as diverse as the relativist claims? And if exceptions to the diversity rule occur, are they due to purely accidental similarities between cultures or to universal characteristics of humans and their societies? Plainly similarities do exist; every culture is reported to have taboos against incest, for example, and against wanton killing within one's in-group. Anthropologist Clyde Kluckhohn has documented such universal elements.[2] Even where particular moral practices and rules vary, universal *areas* of value related to human needs can readily be identified: life and health, economic sufficiency, marriage and family. Is this purely accidental? Is there not some common basis for such similarities?

The diversity thesis further fails to distinguish diversity in particular moral practices from diversity in the principles implicit in such concerns. Practices, like moral rules, are guided by more general concerns. Thus, how societies define property rights and how they punish wrongdoers can vary greatly, but they may still be equally concerned about both conserving property and punishing offenders, and equally concerned about an ordered society. Diversity seems to be more widespread in specific application than in principle.

William Frankena argues that many uncritical beliefs might well change with more adequate information and moral enlightenment, reducing significantly the ethical diversity relativists describe.[3] Consider, for example, what has happened to cannibalism and slavery, and the effect of moral persuasion and legal sanctions on racial and sexual discrimination. At least some of the diversity has yielded to reasonable persuasion. From a Christian perspective this is specially noteworthy, inasmuch as the effects of sin corrupt conduct and distort judgment in ways that the light of truth might correct.

Notice, too, the impracticality of relativism when cultures conflict. If all morality is relative, then what moral objection could one make to the Nazi holocaust, to the economic deprivation of a Latin American under class, or to a militaristic nation's unleashing nuclear devastation on others? And what would be wrong with conducting painful experiments on young children, using them for case studies on the long-term psychological effects of mutilation? In a world where no moral court of appeals exists, might makes right. The only appeal can be to power, unless we can find a basis for coexistence in common concerns and values.

The diversity thesis, then, badly overstates both the variety and the extent of ethical relativity. In any case it in no way implies either that moral practices *ought* to vary as they do or that moral beliefs cannot be true independently of how people actually behave.

The Dependency Thesis

Relativists like the anthropologist cited above hold to the dependency thesis; that is, that morality is not a matter of independent rational judgment but is causally dependent on cultural context. Therefore the particular morality of a people cannot be other than it is: the truth or falsity of their moral beliefs does not really arise.

Suppose I was brought up in a rural community to believe that animals have equal rights with humans to life, liberty and property. That background, no matter how influential or widespread, implies nothing about the truth or falsity of my belief. Or suppose that under Eastern influences you come to believe in the sacredness of cows so that their right to life, liberty and food must take precedence over any human need. Those influences say nothing about the truth or falsity of your belief. Our beliefs may be culturally important and they may be quite dear to us, so that violations of them would be both psychologically and socially upsetting, but not even these reinforcers can vouch for truth or falsity. The dependency thesis, like the diversity thesis, is in effect irrelevant to the question of truth.

But this bites two ways. If beliefs in general are culturally determined, then so is belief in the dependency thesis: it, too, is caused by influences we cannot control. Perhaps it is a useful scientific convention, but that has no more to do with its truth than the thesis itself has to do with the truth of moral beliefs.

Precisely what does the dependency thesis claim? Does it assert that all our beliefs are culture-dependent, or only some? Just as the diversity thesis appears overstated if it claims that no moral beliefs are universal, so the dependency thesis appears overstated if it claims that all moral beliefs are completely dependent on cultural conditions. For then no society could have independently minded moral dissidents, *and* no prophets could arise as preachers of a social justice hitherto unknown. . . . Independent critical reflection breaks the monopoly of cultural determinants. Yet if not all moral beliefs are culturally determined, but some are formed by critical and rational activity, then not all beliefs are as culturally relative as was claimed. If the dependency thesis is pared down to size, relativism does not follow; and if relativism does not follow, then we may ask the truth-question about moral beliefs after all.

What is really at stake in the dependency thesis is the question of freedom and determinism: whether and to what extent we are able to transcend diverse environmental influences on our beliefs by means of critical and imaginative thinking.[4] Interestingly, our initial quotation precludes that possibility by insisting that folkways develop and are modified at an entirely prereflective level, whereas classical views of freedom regard the development of rational self-examination as a prerequisite to freedom from environmental controls. It is hard to believe that even primitive cultures never engage in reflective self-scrutiny, or that their reflection in no way affects behavior patterns. Certainly in developed cultures such reflection occurs in legislatures, educational institutions, churches and the media; and certainly such activities have affected patterns of moral behavior.

Ethnocentrism

At this stage in the debate our cultural relativist is likely to use an

ad hominem argument, accusing advocates of universal, normative moral beliefs of wearing cultural blinders. We argue as we do
because our own culture has so conditioned us; we regard our
own morality as superior and our more rational approach as the
best. We are ethnocentric. Our supposed intolerance is now the
issue, while cultural relativism has become a front supporting
toleration of ethical differences.

But this new argument runs into problems. In the first place, I
may well defend universal moral norms without defending my
own culture. In fact, the Christian will often find herself in that
situation if she consistently follows the example of the biblical
prophets who exposed the moral failures of their own people.
Ethnocentrism is not the only alternative to cultural relativism.

In the second place, the relativist cannot consistently reject all
intolerance. In tolerating other moralities than his own, he must
tolerate their intolerance. Yet he has already come out against
intolerance. Somehow he needs to be both tolerant and intolerant
of it. He can only accomplish that by being selective about whose
intolerance he tolerates, and under what conditions, so that there
are limits to moral tolerance after all. Further, at least one virtue,
tolerance, is then not entirely relative; and at least one moral belief, the belief that we ought to be tolerant, is taken to be true.

The Christian meantime should be as anxious as anybody to
reject intolerance, or at least to be selective in what she tolerates
where cultures differ. The Bible, written over a long span of
human history, speaks of cultures that change, interact and inter-
fuse. Christian ethics also has a long history spanning vast cultural changes, and nowadays it is taking serious stock of Third
World cultures. The Western believer has roots in at least two
moral traditions, an earthly cultural realm (which the New Testament calls "the world") and a heavenly realm. The heavenly
is present now in earthly culture, not conforming to this world
but embodying itself in it and so seeking to enlighten and renew
it. The believer therefore stands, like the biblical prophet, as

An excellent statement

a critic of culture, for she seeks a kingdom that in its fullness is yet to come. Her biblical perspective teaches her to tolerate cultural differences, but it also teaches limitations to ethical tolerance.[5]

A Response to Relativism

The case for cultural relativism, then, is far from complete. Both the diversity thesis and the dependency thesis appear irrelevant to the truth or falsity of moral beliefs, and both are often overstated, seemingly in reaction to the ethnocentric extremes which the Christian also disallows.

Ethical relativism in one form or another is a recurrent position. Protagoras, the Greek Sophist, anticipated the diversity thesis in his famous dictum "a man is the measure of all things." And to Sophist relativism Plato, Aristotle and the Stoics responded by arguing for a universal morality grounded in an unchanging reality. Later Thomas Hobbes, philosopher of the English civil war period, argued that because our self-interest leads to a war of all against all, we must submit to the absolute authority of a ruler. morality then depends on a combination of psychological and social causes. But to this, eighteenth-century moral-sense philosophers like Joseph Butler responded that we are endowed with a faculty for knowing moral truth.[6]

Our response to relativism must also go beyond criticism to the construction of an alternative ethical theory. This I propose to do later in this book. I make no claim that all moral beliefs are in fact held universally. And I make no claim for exceptionless moral rules on every detail of life, or for a legalistic casuistry that prescribes what to do in every circumstance. Rather I shall defend the normative view that there are universal moral principles which ought to be regarded as exceptionless in every culture, and that the moral rules we adopt (sometimes with a needed diversity) should apply those principles to universal areas of human concern and activity.

Holmes' general position,
disclaimer

3
Emotivist Ethics

Moral practices are just emotional responses to our physical and social environment. This thesis, along with cultural relativism, was implicit in the statement cited in the last chapter from anthropologist William Sumner. What happens if this claim is extended to moral beliefs and judgments in developed cultures like our own? Are our beliefs and judgments what they seem on the surface to be, affirmations that are either true or false about the moral worth of something? Or are they, like Sumner's primitive folkways, not cognitive assertions at all but rather emotional expressions?

Ethical emotivism is the view that moral language simply expresses and perhaps arouses emotion, so that nothing we say in moral terms is either true or false about anything. Ethical statements are pseudostatements; they merely vent our feelings or impose them on others, rather than assert something. What we call moral beliefs are really just positive or negative attitudes. "Nuclear war would be utterly immoral" says no more than "Nuclear war? No!" It is just an emotional response to the present situation and its possible consequences. To say something is morally wrong adds nothing at all to rational discussion.

This does not, of course, prevent our making statements about people's attitudes, as journalists, pollsters and sociologists do. Nor does it preclude statements about my own subjective feelings. I can even describe various ways in which ethical terms like *right* and *good* function. But moral judgments are not possible because the ethical terms they use have no reference or meaning. Distinguish the following ways of speaking:

1. A sociological statement about a community's attitude: "Public drunkenness is unacceptable in Smithsburg."

2. A psychological statement about my inner feelings: "I feel bad about what I have done."

3. A linguistic statement about the function of words: "*Right* serves to give approval, while *wrong* disapproves."

4. A normative ethical statement: "Shoplifting is wrong."

The emotivist allows that statements of the first three kinds may be empirically true, but claims that the fourth kind of expression states nothing at all, and so it can be neither true nor false. Rather it vents some negative attitudes and feelings. "Shoplifting is wrong" says no more than "Shoplifting! Oh, no!"

Before we probe this view further, it is important to distinguish emotivism from *ethical subjectivism,* which takes our normative ethical statements to be veiled statements about inner feelings. The subjectivist views statement four above as no different from two. The emotivist says an ethical judgment expresses or *vents* feelings; the subjectivist says it *describes* them. We shall return to this distinction shortly.

The Emotivist's Reasons

What lies behind the emotivist's claim? What would lead someone to reject not only our common reading of moral discourse,

but the entire tradition of Western ethics from both Judeo-Christian and Greek sources as well? In part the reason may be the persistence of unresolved moral arguments, for we seem never to settle whether war is morally wrong, or whether reverse discrimination is just. And how would we go about settling such questions? What are moral beliefs about anyway? What kinds of facts are moral facts, if they are so hard to agree on, so hard apparently to discover? Are they facts at all, or do our arguments amount to nothing but a rhetorical play on feelings?

The rise of emotivism in the first half of the century was connected with two philosophical developments. First, it was a reaction against an attempt to settle moral disputes by appealing to a supposedly universal ethical intuition. This position, popularized in Britain by the "Bloomsbury Circle," was developed by G. E. Moore. He claimed that we recognize the good directly through reflection, and that it is found most fully in things like friendship and aesthetic experience.[1] But this seemed far too provincial a view, far too likely to endorse culturally relative values, and in any case the intuitionists constantly disagreed among themselves. So the emotivists concluded that ethical intuitions really express subjective feelings rather than evidencing a direct knowledge of moral properties or ethical truths.

A second development was the rise of logical positivism with its insistence that only two kinds of cognitive language are possible: analytic statements (like definitions and tautologies) and factual statements that can be empirically tested. Conventional definitions of ethical terms they could therefore allow, as well as psychological or sociological accounts. But moral judgments are not definitions and therefore are not analytic; nor are they empirically verifiable, for right and wrong, good and bad, are not empirically observable properties. Utilitarians like John Stuart Mill had defined "good" as what produces happiness, but how can facts about consequences tell us what is really good? Since moral judgments are neither empirical nor analytic, therefore, the positivists concluded that they cannot be cognitive at all; they must be noncognitive utterances, used to express and arouse emotion.[2]

In the 1930s logical positivism's ethic was facetiously called the "Boo-Hurrah" theory: moral disapproval amounts to booing someone, and approval to cheering him on. C. S. Lewis attacks it in *The Abolition of Man,* pointing out that on this account of values the poet's words about a sublime waterfall do not really mean that the waterfall has sublime aesthetic qualities; rather they express the poet's sublime feelings about it. Likewise my moral condemnation of nuclear war says nothing true or false about nuclear war, but just vents my feelings about it and possibly influences others.

When we argue about moral issues, however, to what do our arguments appeal? We must be debating something. Recognizing the force of this objection, emotivist C. L. Stevenson distinguished some factual beliefs involved in moral arguments from the emotive attitudes.[3] The former have to do with the facts in a case which can be described in empirical language: we argue, for instance, about the consequences of nuclear war in physical, economic and political terms. Our attitudes to the facts, however, find expression in emotive language that has a dynamic effect on others rather than being descriptive or informative. The descriptive term *Russian* might give way to the emotive term *Red,* just as the descriptive *elderly lady* gives way to the emotive *old maid* or *old hag*. Emotive terms influence people's attitudes and so do ethical terms like *right* and *wrong* and *morally unthinkable*. Such words express and affect attitudes and feelings. Thus U.S. nuclear policy evokes a certain interest and emotional response from me, but it might elicit a different response from you—or none at all. In arguing about it, our only cognitive disagreement can be about describable facts, but we also use "moral" language to influence each other's attitudes and reactions.

Stevenson seems to take for granted the underlying behavioristic account of language, that words are links in a cause-effect chain which locks us in to certain reactions. Moral appraisal is a causally determined feeling, an involuntary response to either the situation or the language confronting us. Moral judgments as such are therefore illusory, not judgments at all in reality, for to call something "morally wrong" says nothing true or false.

An Appraisal

Lest we react negatively to this view in an uncritically emotional way, it is important to remember that moral matters are indeed highly charged emotionally and that ethical language carries a lot of emotional freight. God thundered from Sinai when he gave Israel the Law. And we do much more with our ethical discourse than state objective judgments. We instruct, reprimand, advise, prescribe, protest, denounce, warn, plead. The question is not whether moral language is emotionally charged, nor even whether it is ever used to persuade or manipulate. The question is rather whether the only cognitive element in our discussions is descriptive of the empirical facts in moral situations, and not also evaluative.

Can what is distinctively ethical ever be cognitive? I think so, and as a Christian I think it tremendously important to insist that it is *true,* for instance, that we should love our neighbor as ourselves. How shall we argue the matter? First of all, I want to maintain that emotivism (the noncognitive view) implies ethical subjectivism (a cognitive view). To that end, consider what Stevenson regards as the causal power of moral language in the following uses of ethical terms:

1. A moral judgment: "That is wrong."
2. Reporting a moral judgment: "Mom says that is wrong."
3. A statement about language: "*Right* and *wrong* have no cognitive meaning."

Where does the causal influence reside? I suggest that statement one exercises causal power not merely because of the word *wrong* as such, but because of the speaker, his forcefulness or reputation or authority. Likewise the causal power in statement two is due more to Mom's authority or reputation than to the word *wrong*. Baby brother Billy might say the same thing and be ignored. In statement three the ethical terms have no causal power at all.

If the influence of ethical terms depends on the persons using them, then the influence is theirs and that of their moral attitudes rather than of language alone. "That is wrong" translates into "My strong feelings are against it." And "Mom says . . ." asserts something about her. This is ethical subjectivism, a cognitive position. Yet if emotivism implies subjectivism, then moral judgments are not just emotive expressions but are also at least true or false statements about subjective attitudes. They might be about even more than that, as the following (and second) argument implies.

We noted that the rise of emotivist ethics several decades ago was connected to the positivist view of cognitive meaning as either analytic or purely empirical. In the intervening years it has become plain that such a view is extremely hard to defend, and philosophers have argued convincingly against it. Descriptive statements, they point out, are not fully verifiable because interpretive elements creep in with the language we employ. Choosing whether to speak of the "American Revolution" or the "revolt of the American colonies" (as British texts sometimes do), we plainly interpret as we speak. Even in the natural sciences facts are now said to be theory-laden. The much-touted empirical language is not wholly descriptive after all, but also interpretive.[4]

If this is true, then it is not surprising that ethical statements are not empirically verifiable. *Right* and *wrong* are not empirical terms denoting empirically observable qualities, but neither are they just emotivisms. They are evaluative, interpretive terms which refer to nonempirical concepts of rightness or wrongness. The positivist could never admit that because of his theory of meaning. But if that theory is mistaken, then we can admit nonempirical concepts, and ethical judgments may be cognitive after all.

A third argument against emotivism arises when we look more closely at the subjective dispositions, attitudes and interests which emotivism supposes moral language to express. Are they altogether noncognitive, or do interests and attitudes and emotional expressions say something about the objective situations to which they respond, at least about situations as we perceive them? If I cry "That's terrible!" then you know it is potentially a terror-evoking situation and investigate accordingly. If I object to something, saying "That's unjust," then you look for inequities of some sort, for you take *unjust* as an evaluative term tied to certain kinds of situations.[5]

But, after we peel away emotive expression and reference to empirically describable facts, the question still remains: what do ethical terms convey? To what, other than the observable facts associated, for instance, with "inequity," do they refer? Of what are they true or false? If they refer to evaluative *concepts,* used analogously to scientific concepts in classifying and interpreting data, then are these concepts simply about the subjective attitudes of social groups, or do they refer to something external to us, something both extra-mental and extra-linguistic? To answer such questions is in part what an ethical theory is about. Before developing what I take to be a more adequate theory consonant with Christian belief, therefore, we shall look at two cognitive theories, egoism and utilitarianism, which attempt to locate the reference of ethical terms in human experience.

4

Ethical
Egoism

*I*n the last chapters we examined two positions which, if followed consistently, undermine the possibility of truth in ethics. We now move to two popular and influential ethical approaches which base moral decisions on what will maximize certain consequences of a policy or an action. *Egoism* considers only the consequences for oneself, while *utilitarianism* considers the consequences for people at large. We must ask, among other things, whether reducing moral judgments to the question of maximizing benefits for oneself or for people generally is adequate for a consistent and workable ethic, particularly a Christian ethic. We shall look at egoism in this chapter and utilitarianism in the next.

It is difficult to overstate the pervasiveness of ethical egoism in our society. We are familiar with it in teen-agers' struggling to establish an identity of their own and in the enticements offered us daily by the advertising industry. Slogans like "Live it up!" and

"Go for the gusto!" are simply today's versions of the ancient egoist's "Eat, drink and be merry." These forms of it are marks of hedonism, the pursuit of my own pleasure as my highest and all-encompassing good.

Another form is the narcissism which dotes on one's own body, putting physical health and appearance before all else. Or again, self-fulfillment is the accepted goal and has become the focus of an entire approach to psychological counseling.[1] How strangely idealistic it is for finite and fallen beings in a messed-up world like ours to think that fulfillment is perfectly possible! How insulated can the egoist be from desperate problems of people the world over? Yet this is the "me-generation," whose individualism bears tragic fruit—especially in marriage and the family, where interdependence, common goals and mutual service are indispensable.

Novelist Ayn Rand has popularized egoism in political and economic affairs;[2] and it is, I think, no exaggeration to say that self-centered nationalism in any country's policies is simply a kind of corporate egoism. Religion too can become a means to an individual's selfish ends, something which C. S. Lewis's Screwtape took ready advantage of in seducing professed believers. Today evangelical Christianity is sometimes billed as the path, if not to personal affluence, at least to fulfillment, happiness and much else that I might desire for myself. Egoism runs rampant.

Psychological Egoism

What makes ethical egoism so attractive? Undoubtedly, it is the fact that in all of us there runs a strain of self-centeredness: we are motivated at least in part by our own self-interest. Psychological egoism seizes on this fact and generalizes so as to claim that all people are continually motivated by self-interest. The ethical egoist argues that, if people are motivated by self-interest anyway, then they ought to pursue their own good as deliberately and effectively as they can. Notice here the step from psychological "fact" to ethical "ought," from a description to a normative obligation.

In the first place, one cannot draw a normative conclusion directly from a descriptive premise alone. By itself, apart from some other additional premise, "is" does not imply "ought." The egoist is likely to respond that while no direct inference is possible, ethical egoism is still the most naturally acceptable approach since we are all psychological egoists anyway. His step from "is" to "ought" is not necessarily intended as a logical inference, but more as a recognition of the psychological status quo.

In the second place, then, we must question the status quo. Is psychological egoism altogether true? If it is put forward as a universally valid description, then we need only one counterexample to deny it, one nonegoistical person or at least one nonegoistical action. The supreme counterexample, of course, is Jesus Christ with his self-giving love. But the egoist can respond that unselfish acts may still be in one's own interest and may provide a great deal of satisfaction, ego-fulfillment and other long-term rewards. Citing examples of unselfishness therefore is not enough to convince us.

Indeed the Bible significantly appeals to our self-interest regarding both the consequences of belief or unbelief and the consequences of our actions. Its rewards and punishments appeal to an egoistical motivation. The question we must ask then is whether psychological egoism tells the *whole* story, whether self-interest is our sole motivation or even the overriding one. Does concern for our own welfare really outweigh concern for anyone or anything else?

The eighteenth-century Bishop Joseph Butler responded that while I do indeed desire my own inner happiness in general, motivation is tied in specific cases to particular external objects.[3] I do not want food for the sake of my own happiness in general, but because I am hungry and need it to go on working, perhaps to go on serving others. A husband does not want sex just for its maximum pleasure but because he loves his wife and values closeness to her. The desire for food or sex may be self-referential, but it is not self-confined, not purely and solely egoistical.[4] This is the difference between what Butler calls true self-love and unnatural or debauched self-love. Debauched self-love separates the things we value for their own sake from the pleasure they afford, thereby indulging itself in ways that may be counterproductive to true self-interest.

Another important psychological fact now arises: the "hedonic paradox" that the pursuit of pleasure for its own sake often results not in pleasure but frustration. Parallels exist with regard to other forms of egoism as well, so that we can speak of the "fulfillment paradox" and the "egoism paradox." Concentration on maximizing self-fulfillment can so distract our attention from enriching activities and external objects that the sense of fulfillment slips through our fingers. Aesthetic and intellectual pursuits require a high degree of detachment and disciplined attention to an object, and so are notoriously unsatisfying for the debauched. Observe this paradox in its classic statement by the Hebrew poet.

I said to myself, "Come now, I will make a test of pleasure; enjoy yourself." But behold, this also was vanity. I said of laughter, "It is mad," and of pleasure, "What use is it?" I searched with my mind how to cheer my body with wine—my mind still guiding me with wisdom—and how to lay hold on folly, till I might see what was good for the sons of men to do under heaven during the few days of their life. I made great works; I built houses and planted vineyards for myself; I made myself gardens and parks, and planted in them all kinds of fruit trees. I made myself pools from which to water the forest of growing trees. I bought male and female slaves, and had slaves who were born in my house; I had also great possessions of herds and flocks, more than any who had been before me in Jerusalem. I also gathered for myself silver and gold and the treasure of kings and provinces; I got singers, both men and women, and many concubines, man's delight.

So I became great and surpassed all who were before me in Jerusalem; also my wisdom remained with me. And whatever my eyes desired I did not keep from them; I kept my heart from no pleasure, for my heart found pleasure in all my toil, and this was my reward for all my toil. Then I considered all that my hands had done and the toil I had spent in doing it, and behold, all was vanity and a striving after wind, and there was nothing to be gained under the sun. (Eccles 2:1-11)

True self-love, on the other hand, does not conflict with loving people and things for their own sake. A good novel or play, a symphony, a research project or a good conversation can capture and hold my interest and, as it were, "take me out of myself." Consider also friendship, marriage, parenthood: they naturally develop in us nonegoistical motivations to such an extent that we will sacrifice our own interests for those we love. We desire their well-being as much and sometimes more than our own. The Bible tells us to love our neighbors *as ourselves,* and a husband is to love his wife *as his own body* (Lk 10:27; Eph 5:28). Self-love is properly matched by love for others, Butler insisted, and it no more conflicts with benevolence than it does with love for God. Psychologically, this seems much closer to the overall picture than the self-confined love of psychological egoism.

Some have held that it is overly optimistic to talk about natural benevolence in fallen human beings, that Thomas Hobbes was more to the point when he pictured our psychological egoism as leading to the war of all against all.[5] Butler may well have absorbed too much Enlightenment optimism, it is true, but on the other hand we must still recognize the common grace of God which preserves society from turning its back altogether on benevolent concerns and plunging wholesale into the depths of debauched egoism. Every good thing, not least the love of parent for child and the concern people show for peace and justice on this earth, comes ultimately from God. There is no need to stress our need for God by exaggerating our egoism.

Psychological egoism, it then seems, is a mistaken view. Not only can apparent exceptions to the rule be cited, but human motivation is more complex than egoism allows. Self-interest is not the whole story, but coexists with altruistic concerns. Egoistic motives do not always override all else; in fact, by themselves they are often counterproductive. As a steppingstone to ethical egoism, psychological egoism fails.

Is Ethical Egoism Viable?

What sort of social order would be required if conflicting self-interests are to be brought together in some sort of peaceable and orderly way? In the context of the English civil war, Thomas Hobbes was utterly pessimistic about egoism left to itself, uncontrolled; he saw human life in that condition as "nasty, short and brutish." Enlightened self-interest, he argued, requires that individual liberties be surrendered to a benevolent monarch with absolute power. But if psychological egoism were true, would the absolute monarch really be benevolent or would his own self-interest override the interests of those entrusted to his care? Can egoism work—if it is egoism without exception even in those who rule?

In the *Republic,* Plato proposed to train a ruling class in whom egoism could not take root. Their genetic inheritance, education and socialization would all be so arranged, their economic and sexual needs so fully supplied, that self-interest would not distract their minds from truths and justice. Only with nonegoistical rulers, he maintained, is a just society possible.

The eighteenth-century Enlightenment was more optimistic. The French Baron de Mandeville likened humanity to a swarm of bees, each pursuing its own ends, yet by nature composing a harmonious and peaceable realm. Adam Smith's "invisible hand" was able to function because a natural benevolence combines with our natural self-interest. Karl Marx, however, saw no hope for a peaceable or just society until the conflicting self-interests of social classes are overcome in an eventual classless society.

The question social philosophy poses, then, is whether egoism can provide a viable ethic or whether it leads to anarchy. Can the ethical egoist be trusted to do what is good for others? To consider this question more closely, we shall distinguish two kinds of egoism. The individual egoist says she should seek always and only her own individual good, and everyone should so serve her in particular. The universal egoist says that *every* individual should seek always and only his or her own good.

Consider Sally, an individual egoist. Who would listen to her advice? Sally will only advise me to do what is in her own self-interest, using me as fully as she can for her own ends. If I ask what I ought to do for my own good, she in effect tells me to serve her ends, even though that may not help me. Even if she advises me to be an egoist too, I will have to conclude she does so for her own benefit; to take her advice I may have to reject it. Sally can give no objective counsel, can make no disinterested judgments. She cannot even make me an egoist like herself. She should never be trusted, except to pursue her own interests regardless of the cost to others. Nobody would want to elect Sally to public office. And who would want to marry her?

To avoid this impasse, the individual egoist would likely become a universal egoist like her friend Bill and advise each of us to seek his own individual good. But can I trust Bill any more than I do Sally? For if each seeks his or her own good, so too does Bill when he gives advice, and we are back in Sally's grasp. If we take Bill's advice at face value, then we create Mandeville's swarm of bees, so unrealistic in its idealism, and we are likely to end up, as Hobbes put it less optimistically, with a war of all against all.

While individual egoism retreats to universal egoism, then, universal egoism collapses into anarchy—that is, unless Bill and Sally and all the rest of us can be made to work for the common good. To suppose that somehow, without our forsaking egoism,

nature or providence will work all things together for good, independent of our efforts, takes considerable credulity in light of
human history and our sinfulness. If we think universal egoism
would not be so bad as to create anarchy but would rather make
life into a stimulating competitive sport, then there must be rules
to the game, natural laws we all obey willy-nilly. This again takes
credulity. Moreover, if natural laws do hold our egoism in check,
then psychological egoism does not have the last word after all,
and the ethical egoist's basis is lost.

Individual egoism retreats into universal egoism, and universal
egoism collapses into anarchy. Egoism seemingly fails as a consistent and workable ethic. It should be noted, however, that this
line of criticism depends on the assumption that self-interest can
indeed get out of hand and become destructive of others. Hobbes
took this point of view, possibly because he was influenced by the
biblical doctrine of sin, possibly because he lived amid conflicts
that tore seventeenth-century England apart. Broad church thinkers did not share his pessimistic view of human nature, however,
holding to a more natural moral order in human society, more
natural altruism and benevolence. But this means rejecting both
psychological and ethical egoism. Some utilitarians claim that I
should seek good consequences for all people because that is what
will make *me* happy: they adopt utilitarian means to egoistical
ends. But that does not justify their egoistic ends, even if it does
keep them from bestiality or anarchy. And the adequacy of a utilitarian approach must itself be considered.

What can we conclude about egoism from a Christian standpoint? First, we observed that while a legitimate psychological
self-interest is assumed in Scripture, it is balanced by ethical concern for others. All persons are created in God's image of equal
worth: the Christian must love her neighbor as she does herself.
Second, egoism views people much more individualistically than
does Scripture. In the Bible people are considered in relation to
others—as members of families, of the community of faith, or of

nations—and their responsibilities are largely those of these groups. We shall come back to this point subsequently. Third, the doctrine of human depravity must be balanced by the doctrine of common grace: that is, God in his goodness restrains the evil possibilities inherent in a degenerate egoism, maintaining a degree of order in both nature and society to bear witness to himself as Creator and Lawgiver.

Finally, neither egoism nor altruism, nor even a balance of the two, suffices to describe an overall biblical ethic. The highest end is rather to glorify God and enjoy him forever, to seek first the kingdom of God. The highest motivation is love for God: true neighbor-love and true self-love properly follow from this. And both of them logically lead us back to their source in love for God.

5

Utilitarianism

While the egoist pursues his own self-interest, the utilitarian is concerned to maximize the benefits for the maximum number of people. In one form or another, this has been probably the most influential ethical approach in English-speaking philosophy during the twentieth century. Its attraction, I think, is severalfold. In the first place, it still appeals to self-interest in that most of us, of course, stand to benefit by the maximizing of good consequences for society at large.

In the second place, utilitarianism was originally addressed to social policy, as a basis for penal reform and for legislation. Currently it is of keen interest in economics.[1] In effect, the rise of utilitarianism has been tied to the rise of the empirical social sciences. If we can develop empirical generalizations or "covering laws" about the consequences of a certain kind of legislation, economic policy or form of punishment, then we should be able also to make decisions which maximize the good consequences and minimize the bad. In regard to punishment, for example, Jeremy Bentham argued from the supposedly empirical generalization that a potential criminal will act so as to maximize the pleasure associated with his action and minimize the pain. If we ensure enough pain to outweigh the pleasure, we should then be able to deter him from criminal action.

The question we must address before exploring such applications, however, is whether the utilitarian principle is sufficient for an adequate and workable ethic, particularly a Christian ethic. Can moral judgments properly be reduced to the question of maximizing benefits?

Needed: One Nonconsequential Judgment
If we desire an action A_1 to facilitate A_2, then to be entirely consequentialist we must have chosen A_2 to facilitate A_3, and likewise A_3 for the sake of A_4 and A_4 for the sake of A_5, and so on. But a chain of consequences that has no end is absurd: why choose that chain and not another? A decision is needed as to which set of consequences to prefer, a decision that cannot be based entirely on consequences because that would take us back again to the infinite regress. A nonconsequential decision is therefore needed as to the *kind* of consequence we are to seek. The *quality* of consequence is really the decisive thing, not just the quantity; and in actuality the utilitarian wants to maximize consequences of a certain kind, *good* consequences rather than bad. But deciding what consequences to regard as good is itself a nonconsequential judgment.

Bentham took the good to be pleasure. He was a hedonist. But pleasure is a general and vague concept, and hedonism makes it sound as if we were just passive beings, either pained or pleased. Mill therefore qualifies it, preferring the higher pleasures (aesthetic and intellectual, for instance) to the lower, physical ones. Better a human dissatisfied, he claimed, than a pig satisfied.

Two difficulties surface immediately. First, Bentham says he chooses pleasure because in fact everyone seeks pleasure. But this poses the "is-ought" problem again: we cannot directly deduce any "ought" from an empirical generalization alone. Second, why prefer higher pleasures? Mill's choice is not a purely consequential matter, but appeals to the dignity and desirability of what is distinctive about humans. Later utilitarians like G. E. Moore took the good to be an intuitive concept, not empirically defined, whose scope extends to a wide variety of cultural and social satisfactions which we seek for their own sake. Here again is a nonconsequential basis. In effect, the question of *which* consequences are good is always answered on nonconsequentialist grounds.

Suppose that the utilitarian has settled this question and now wants to maximize consequences of the sort he has decided are good. He now faces a second problem: how shall we calculate consequences?

Calculating Consequences

Bentham proposed a "hedonic calculus." For each alternative action or policy, we can quantify the pleasure involved in terms of its intensity, duration, certainty or uncertainty, propinquity or remoteness, fecundity, purity (no admixture of pain) and extent (the number of persons affected). Then we can likewise quantify the pain and simply subtract the sum of pain from the sum of pleasure. At this point it should be easy to identify the path of maximum surplus pleasure.

Is it that easy, however? Mill's qualitative distinction between kinds of pleasures forced him to reject Bentham's calculus: quality is not reducible to quantity. The prior question is, what *kind* of pleasure do we want? And if not pleasure, then what other kind of good are we after? Can that be completely quantified?

Precisely what consequences should we consider in the calculation? Should we include only the intended consequences of an action, or other predictable consequences also, or just the actual consequences? The last of these will not help us make judgments in advance. As to the first, are intended consequences alone enough? Should not other predictable outcomes be weighed too? But our empirical predictions concerning social consequences and human happiness are extremely limited in both their extent and their probability. Consider the unforeseen effects of high-rise public housing in our cities, for instance, and of where and how we store waste chemicals like dioxin. Just how probable should a consequence be before it is taken into account? Why should more weight be given to immediate consequences (propinquity) than to more distant ones (for instance, in regard to the disposal of nuclear waste or the use of scarce resources)? Do we bear "negative responsibility" for consequences we allow by doing nothing?

To make judgments that involve calculations of these sorts is at best a complex matter, subject to varying decisions about what consequences to weigh and how much weight to give each. All of this assumes that we know how to objectively evaluate the consequences under consideration, an assumption which is dubious given the disagreements over what is really "good."

Yet that is not the only problem in making utility calculations work. In light of the vast complexity of utilitarian calculations, should everybody try to make decisions this way—every business person, investor, physician, politician, parent, social worker, voter? Or should utilitarian calculations be left to the few knowledgeable experts with access to all the statistics and detailed scenarios bearing on the decision? It appears that the more practicing utilitarians we have, the less the overall utility; and the fewer utilitarians there are in the world, the greater the utility! Utilitarianism is hardly an ethic for everyone.

The Problem of Distributive Justice

What does it mean to "maximize the good"? Is it enough to take the *sum* of all the surplus of good over bad for all the people involved? Or should we *average* it all across an entire population?

Or should we consider different segments separately? If 100 people each receive 10 "bens" (units of benefit), then the sum total is 1000 "bens" and the average is 10. But if we increase the benefit for 10 people to 100 bens each, give the next 60 people their original 10 "bens," and the remaining 30 no "bens" at all, then the total benefit is 1000 + 600 + 0 = 1600 "bens"; and the average is up to 16. But the distribution is now extremely unequal. Which of these two is the morally better distribution of benefits?

The example is overly simplified, but it raises questions about distributive justice and equal rights. Does the sum total of well-being justify ignoring inequities? Does an average income tell us all that matters? And can the utility principle by itself tell us how best to *distribute* benefits?

Mill talked at length about *equal* justice. But he still thought it a matter of maximal utility, so that we should respect the rights and liberties of others for the sake of maximizing the common good and only restrict those liberties to avoid harm to others. But is that principle sufficient to ensure equal justice for all?

Consider, for example, the lengths to which a totalitarian state often goes "for the common good." As long as the ultimate appeal is only to the general good, what guarantees minority rights? Does the end justify any means at all? Why not repress dissent? Why not punish the innocent to deter others? Why not let social engineering go on unhampered by scruples about individual rights? What is *morally* wrong in Huxley's *Brave New World* or in C. S. Lewis's *That Hideous Strength*?

Suppose that two acts, A and B, would each produce the same surplus of good over evil consequences. Yet suppose too that A involves breaking a promise or discriminating against a minority while B does not, and that the consequences of these features in A have been figured into the calculation. Then the utilitarian would have no basis for preferring A to B or B to A, despite the fact that common morality would opt unequivocally for B.

Suppose now that A involves a slightly larger balance of good than does B, while still requiring the broken promise or injury to a minority. The utilitarian would then have to choose A over B, even though most people would be quite dubious about that choice.

What utilitarianism lacks is a principle of distributive justice that is not subject to and cannot be manipulated by the principle of utility. William Frankena, therefore, proposes an ethic in which the principle of beneficence (which utilitarians emphasize) is supplemented by an independent principle of justice.[2] John Rawls's highly influential book *A Theory of Justice* argues that a well-ordered society will not only be designed to advance the good of its members, but will also be effectively regulated by a conception of justice as fairness that benefits the least advantaged. Justice must not be subordinated to other goods we want to pursue.

The Problem with Empiricism

It is questionable whether a principle of distributive justice could be supplied by the empirical methods that gave modern utilitarianism birth. The empiricist regards a person as a bundle of experiences, both actual and possible. Mill explicitly took this view, having no place in his thinking for any enduring entity like a mind or soul, and a contemporary utilitarian like J. J. C. Smart adds little to it in his materialistic view of persons.[3] What value, then, has a person to herself other than the satisfaction of experiencing what she experiences, and what value has she to somebody else other than the satisfaction he finds in his experience with her? The value of persons is then measured entirely in terms of people's experiences, individually and collectively, and their actions are evaluated in terms of empirical consequences. The value of a minority, too, is not seen in other terms, such as the intrinsic rights of human beings in God's image, and the value of keeping a promise has nothing to do with moral integrity or respect for persons for their own sake.

Consider further moral integrity. In our earlier example of two actions, A and B, where A involved breaking a promise or discriminating against a minority, the utilitarian concerned himself only with the consequences. Why does common moral sense tend to disagree, saying there is more to discrimination against minorities than its consequences? I suggest it is because moral integrity is involved in how we treat others. I am concerned not only about the beneficial or adverse consequences of my actions, but also about *being just*. If people are more than collections of experiences and of physical causes and effects, and if I am also a responsible moral agent, then respecting the integrity of persons—both myself and others—is important in itself. This is *not* just a matter of consequences, but also of motives and actions and the value of persons.

We can see now the breadth of the problem with empiricism in ethics. It is not just the problem of defining the good, calculating consequences or providing an unwavering basis for distributive justice. It is also the problem of ascribing sufficient value to persons, and so of grounding moral integrity and moral duty. In Immanuel Kant's terms, not all moral imperatives are *hypothetical* ones, related to whatever consequences we may desire: "If you want to succeed and be happy, then work hard." A *categorical* imperative is unconditional. It commands us independently of our desires or utilitarian concerns. We simply *ought* to treat people as ends in themselves and not just as means.

But purely empirical and consequentialist approaches cannot talk to us in such categorical terms. We need what is called a *deontological* element in our ethic, an emphasis on moral obligation that is not simply a function of desires or circumstances. For this we now turn more directly toward a Christian ethic.

6

Toward a
Christian
Ethic

Consequences play an important part in moral decisions, and not least for the Christian. The problems with basing an ethic on consequences *alone* must not blind us to this fact. Christians should be concerned with doing good to others and should doubtless make decisions which contribute to God's purposes in this world. Indeed, some Christians have adopted a kind of utilitarian ethic: in the eighteenth century, for instance, William Paley declared that virtue is "doing good to mankind, in obedience to the will of God, and for the sake of everlasting happiness."[1] And, it has been argued, since God is benevolent we, too, should be benevolent and aim to maximize the good for others. Mill himself likened the utility principle to Jesus' golden rule: do unto others as you would have them do to you.[2] What about this?

Doing Good Deeds
Is doing good deeds all that counts in a Christian ethic? Is love or

benevolence the only moral attribute of God? Is it enough for any ethic? Recall the problem of defining the good. *What* good or goods should we maximize? What is our highest end? From a biblical standpoint it is not human happiness or well-being, not the richest possible package of experiences, for persons are more than bundles of experiences and their value therefore is more. Yet even our value as persons is not ultimate but is derived from God, who created us in his own image. Our highest end, as Jesus said, is to love the Lord our God with all our being, and for his sake to love others as ourselves. It is to seek first *his* kingdom.

In the words of the Westminster Shorter Catechism, our highest end is to glorify God and enjoy him forever (*not* to enjoy *ourselves* as much as we can). A Christian ethic must put this first, and human happiness comes later because both the worth and the possibility of human well-being derive from God. Love for oneself and others is not enough; love for God takes priority, and other loves must flow from it.

Moreover, if love is regarded as a consequentialist principle, then it needs to ground the principle of distributive justice on more than simple utility. Indeed, "do unto others as you would have them do to you" sounds equitable and just as well as loving. God is not only loving; he is also just. These two attributes stand out through the entire biblical record, and neither is reducible to the other. I therefore find attempts at a Christian utilitarianism ill begotten; we need an independent principle of justice to ensure an equitable distribution of good, in addition to the principle of love or benevolence that maximizes good consequences.

Structuring an Ethic

To put this in context, however, we must first relate what I call principles to other ingredients in an ethical theory. Let us distinguish the four ingredients: (1) cases, (2) area rules, (3) principles and (4) bases.

The moral problems we face almost daily have to do with (1) particular *cases:* Is $5 a fair price to charge? Was Mary's abortion morally justified? Should the doctor lie to Grandma about her condition? Would you lie to the Gestapo to save your Jewish neighbor? In addressing such cases, we usually draw on (2) moral *rules* that apply to various areas of life: in the cases cited they would be rules about business transactions, about the value of fetal life and about telling the truth. These rules depend on (3) underlying *principles,* and they apply those principles to various areas of activity. Finally, the principles themselves are logically justified by reference to (4) theological or philosophical *bases,* or presuppositions.

This pattern is discernible in almost any ethic, and we could readily trace it in the biblical materials on morality. Consider, for example, the well-known Ten Commandments in Exodus 20:1-17, which include moral *rules* for major areas of human responsibility: the sanctity of human life and of the marriage relationship, respect for others' property and for the truth. A fascinating array of case applications appears in subsequent chapters in Exodus, *cases* which can be classified under the various rules in the Decalog (the Ten Commandments). The *basis* for these rules is quite explicit: they are commands of God. And the *principles* on which they rest, while implicit in the Exodus account, became explicit elsewhere. The moral law offers an even standard for the kind of just and equitable society preached later by the Old Testament prophets, and the underlying heart of the law is love (Mt 22:34-40; Rom 13:8-10). A similar pattern is evident in other biblical materials, in the Wisdom literature, the Prophets and the New Testament, all of which reiterate the bearing of God's law and its underlying principles on human life.

Moral Principles

Moral principles, the most inclusive and ultimate ethical concepts, apply not just to particular kinds of activities but universally—to every kind of involvement, whatever it may be. They are therefore exceptionless principles which can never give way to something more inclusive and which must never give way to expediency. "What does the Lord require . . . but to do justice, and to love kindness, and to walk humbly with your God?" (Mic 6:8). We are never exempted from acting with justice and love.[3]

In this context, consider these two principles. Both are concerned for persons, justice for their equitable treatment and love for their good (their highest good, that is, not necessarily their enjoyment or success in life). "The LORD works . . . justice for all who are oppressed" (Ps 103:6), and so ought we. Just laws and just government, a just economy with fair prices and fair wages, an equitable relationship between faithful husband and faithful wife, a peaceful and equitable relationship also between the nations of the world: these should be our concern as they are God's (Is 9:2-7; 11:1-5). Justice is the distributive principle which treats all persons equitably.

Love in the biblical sense *(agapē)* is not what the Greeks called *eros,* desiring something for oneself, but is rather a self-giving, sacrificial attitude. Nor is it like the kind of friendship which, according to Aristotle, must always be reciprocated if it is to survive. Nor is it a warm and generous feeling for others. It is rather an overall moral principle, all-inclusive and exceptionless, that should govern all our actions, a selfless devotion to God that issues in sacrificial service to others.

Justice and love do not conflict but contribute each to the other. As love is obligated in justice to distribute its benefits equitably, rather than playing favorites or practicing discrimination and unfairness, so justice is motivated by love to keep its relentless quest tirelessly alive. Justice stresses the right outward ordering of life, while love is more an inner, personalized concern. Love without justice would be amorphous and lack direction. Justice without love would be uncaring and detached. But together they comprise the principles of God's kingdom, summed up in the Hebrew term *shalom*. It means peace, but peace of a certain kind: a just peace (each man sitting under his own fig tree, says Micah), a liberating peace (the children dancing in the streets, says Zechariah), a peace in which all enjoy the bounty of God and honor him thereby. Our highest end is to glorify God and enjoy him forever. Consequently, these principles of God's kingdom are the principles of a Christian ethic, to guide our judgments and our conduct.

Moral Rules

What moral principles require in specified areas of life or kinds of activities is indicated by moral rules. "You shall not kill" (Ex 20:13) calls for the regard for human life expected in a just and equitably ordered society motivated by a love that is not self-serving. But since this is very general and needs more detailed application, the Mosaic law goes on to treat accidental manslaughter, killing in self-defense and capital punishment as exceptional cases which must nonetheless be safeguarded against unjust abuses.

While similar structures are discernible in almost any ethical theory, some ethicists reject a "rule-ethic" and, because they move directly from moral principles to the cases in which we act, adopt an "act-ethic" instead. Rules for them are, at best, rules of thumb, behavior patterns based on past experiences; and we are not at all obligated to follow them. The act-utilitarian, for instance, is prepared to treat each particular killing or each sexual liaison separately, in terms of its utility. This puts considerable strain on our ability to predict and calculate consequences, and it leans strongly toward ethical relativism. Situation ethics is an act-theory in that it treats each situation on its own merits and shuns moral rules as a form of legalism.[4]

An act-ethic presupposes that no universal and lasting structures to human life exist, that there are no distinguishable areas of unchanging responsibility, no "action spheres" we all have in common. But Christian belief in a divinely ordered creation argues otherwise, and theologians speak variously of creation orders, law spheres and creation mandates. The point is that humans are generically alike and share a common world, that we have common needs and common activities—physical, economic, familial and so forth. Situations do not differ so widely as the situationist supposes, nor do acts differ so greatly as the act-ethicist assumes. Moral rules for common areas are therefore not only possible but also extremely valuable in guiding life wisely and well. A Christian ethic especially, with the biblical view of creation in mind and the divine law as its paradigm, will be a rule-ethic.

Nor is this the legalism which situationists fear. Legalism binds the conscience to manmade rules for every possible situation, imposing a rule for every case. It hides the weightier matters of the law, the underlying principles of love and justice, beneath a load of particular behavioral requirements. It elevates its rules to the level of exceptionless principles. But not so a Christian rule-ethic.

Cases

Ethical theories generally have ways of handling exceptional cases that do not fit neatly under the rules. I am not speaking of particulars where no existing moral rules directly apply—as was initially the case, for example, regarding recombinant DNA research. There we back up to more general rules regarding respect for human life and for our genetic heritage and the environment. I am speaking rather of moral dilemmas, where every available alternative seems to violate some moral rule. As a doctor, would you deceive a patient about her probably fatal disease in order to stir the hope she needs to fight it? Would you lie to save a Jewish neighbor from the Gestapo? As a police officer, could you use lethal force to save innocent victims from mob violence? Would you steal the gun from someone threatening suicide? How can we deprive a person of his God-given liberty, in punishment for a crime? And what about a defensive war to resist unjust and unprovoked aggression that threatens the life of a civilian population? To fight is to take human life. Not to fight is to let human life be unjustly taken. In either case evil is done, some of which we could help prevent. What can we do in such moral dilemmas? Are there not here some unavoidable exceptions to moral rules?

The consequentialist will be content to weigh the respective outcomes of alternative actions so as to maximize the good and minimize the evil results. But we have seen that this is not enough, for considerations other than consequences are involved in moral decisions. The alternative is to rank moral rules according to their centrality to one's underlying principles. Thus the sanctity of innocent human life ranks higher than telling the truth to murderous Gestapo agents, in terms of both a just society and sacrificial love. When innocent victims are being unjustly arrested and killed, the unjust killer has no right to expect the truth. And love, in the interest of justice, protects the victims.

Another proposal often accompanies this: formulate rules to govern exceptions to rules. To prevent easy rationalizations of immoral acts in regard to civil disobedience, for instance, Martin Luther King, Jr., was careful to set forth moral limitations: there must be an overwhelmingly just cause in the form of unjustly discriminatory legislation, and those who disobey must be willing to suffer arrest and go to trial in order that the unjust law may be challenged in court. Civil disobedience is selective and limited because it still submits to the authority of law per se. In regard to war, the "just war" theory sets forth conditions under which it would be morally just (and loving, in Christian versions of the theory) to go to war, and it establishes limitations that must then be placed on the conduct and continuation of a conflict.[5] We are never exempted, even in such exceptional cases, from justice and love. We shall pursue this later in regard to some other moral issues.

This sketch of the fourfold structure of an ethic provides a helpful tool both for analyzing ethical positions and for approaching moral decisions. Because bases and principles are plainly more fundamental and strategic than the resultant rules and case decisions, we have examined the egoist and utilitarian *principles* as well as their *bases* in psychological egoism and empiricism, respectively. This structure also gives us a handle on our thinking about Christian ethics, where we can see the relation of overall principles to moral rules. Insofar as Christian and non-Christian ethics differ, they are more likely to differ on principles than in regard to area rules or cases. There they can quite often—not always, of course—make common cause, as they do about nuclear arms reduction or chemical waste disposal. Sometimes they may even agree about justice and love, provided we don't probe too much the theological side of those concepts. But the most insuperable disagreement will be at the most fundamental level— bases.

To round out our thinking about a Christian ethic, two more questions must be faced. In chapter seven we address the question of moral knowledge: how we may know what principles and rules are right, and how we may make properly informed moral decisions. Then in chapter eight we turn to the basis on which all else rests, the basis of moral obligation itself.

7

Moral
Knowledge

*W*e have been talking about moral truth, but how can we know it? We have seen the structure or form that an ethic takes, but what about the content? How do we come to recognize moral principles? How can we discover the moral rules we should follow? How can we test our moral beliefs to be more sure they are correct?

Common Morality

Experience is a great teacher, it is said, accumulating lessons learned from life and passing them on from generation to generation. A traditional wisdom results, that has been tried and tested through the years. The history of jurisprudence acknowledges a common law of this sort, established in social practices rooted in a dim and distant past but still significant enough to be a guide for positive law. Analogously, some people speak of a common morality established by social sentiment over the years and significant enough to be the guide to a more systematic ethic.

It must be acknowledged that the moral wisdom of a culture frequently offers a great deal of lasting value. It has been forged and refined over the course of time amid varied circumstances in the heat of the universal human condition and the unchanging pressures of our common human nature. And similar moral concerns have often been noted in cultures with vastly different histories.[1]

But problems arise. The first concerns the extent of such common morality, for it tends to deal with cases and common areas of life as they have been in the past, a limited array of things in any case, and to lack overall principles from which moral dilemmas and novel moral issues might be addressed. Is piecemeal wisdom a broad-enough basis for a comprehensive ethic? The second problem concerns the finality of common morality: if it has been accumulating over the years, then presumably the process continues, with changes that track the changing moral climate. Common Western morality in the 1980s is markedly different from that of the 1950s, and different again from America of the 1860s. Historical and cultural relativism rears its head. And the Christian in particular would be wary of any moral consensus of an ungodly society in a fallen world.

Several attempts have been made to overcome these obstacles. One of these is the measured empiricism of utilitarians guided by careful generalizations about observable regularities in human behavior, which we analyzed in chapter five. But this, we concluded, is insufficient for defining the good, calculating consequences and ensuring distributive justice. It was supposedly scientific, objective and independent of all nonempirical input, but by itself it yields no oughts, no moral principles other than utility, and is in reality an ethical cul-de-sac, a dead-end street.

Conscience
Another attempt to overcome the limitations of a common moral-

ity, one developed by eighteenth-century "moral sense" philosophers, maintained that we are all endowed by God with a specifically moral faculty which balances our natural tendency to self-love with an additional tendency to benevolence.[2] Some thought this moral faculty was a distinctive sentiment or feeling. Francis Hutcheson thought that an aesthetic appreciation for altruism offsets our egoism, while Lord Shaftesbury claimed that we feel pleasure when the two harmonize. Others regarded the moral sense as a cognitive faculty: denying I ought to keep a promise, for instance, is to say that a promise is not a promise, and that is self-contradictory. Bishop Butler labeled this kind of moral faculty "conscience."[3]

But the two problems of common morality persist. The moral faculty (conscience, if you will) has only a limited range of operation, and on many matters we likely "have no conscience." Moreover it varies significantly from person to person and culture to culture, seeming to depend on moral training and cultural conditioning as much as anything—as psychologists are quick to point out. Again relativism raises its head. Where then is the reliability of moral knowledge?

Note that Butler's use of conscience for a universal moral faculty hardly coincides with the biblical usage. In Scripture, a person's conscience can be weak, seared or defiled, and where it prods and pricks depends on how it is informed and shaped. It may indeed be informed by the biblical record of God's law or by nature's witness to the moral law (Rom 2:14-16), but it may also be sadly misinformed. Conscience in and of itself is a variable, unsure and often defective guide. If we take the term literally (Greek *syneidēsis*), it simply means a capacity to put things together and make judgments.

What then are we to make of the idea of a moral faculty? It represents a dated faculty psychology. It also seems an overly ambitious theory if it does not reconcile our moral differences. In fact, William Frankena suggests that such a faculty simply indicates a "moral point of view" we take in caring about issues and wanting to make rational judgments about them in a personally disinterested way.[4] In itself it provides neither a substantive moral principle (like justice), nor moral rules, nor judgments about particular actions.

Intuitionism

Twentieth-century intuitionists take a somewhat different tack, locating the common moral sense in relation not to particular acts but to an overall moral principle. G. E. Moore claimed that our intuition is of the good in a utilitarian sense,[5] and W. D. Ross that it is of the right (the deontological principle).[6] Granted that basic intuition, further moral guidance can be derived—whether for good ends to seek or for right rules to follow.

Again two main criticisms can be leveled. First, the moral intuition is sufficiently unclear that radical differences arise among people's intuitions. Second, we are not told what makes the good good or the right right. Ross allows that in some sense moral obligation is part of the structure of the universe, but this needs to be spelled out in a way that justifies his conclusions as to what is right.

Duty for Duty's Sake

Taking as his starting point the common idea that only a good will is good without qualification, Immanuel Kant argued that good will excludes willing something either because of its desirable consequences or because of our own inclinations. Nor is it enough to act just in accordance with duty; we must act *out of* regard for duty and respect for moral law.[7] This is a universal and necessary moral principle, and from it Kant develops various formulations of his famous categorical imperative. We should always act from maxims (rules), he says, that can without self-contradiction be universalized. For example, a needy student might promise to repay a loan without any intention of doing so.

But if this became a universal rule, nobody would ever make student loans. This guiding maxim would be self-contradictory, and should not be adopted in the first place. But this is a negative criterion which can only disqualify some things and rule them wrong. It cannot function positively in telling us what is right: we can bring candidates to the bar of reason, but we cannot derive moral rules for ourselves. Kant's further formulation, "always treat persons as ends and not just as means," is stated positively enough and can be very fruitful, but as it stands it, too, is not sufficient. To derive from it, for example, a full human rights theory that respects whatever is essential to personhood would additionally require definition of the essential characteristics of the human person.[8]

Kant's perception of the need for a deontological principle is to be appreciated, as is his emphasis on right motivation and the inherent value of persons. But further objections have been raised to his extreme confidence in the person of good will and what is rationally derivable therefrom. In moral matters especially we have mixed motives and a vast capacity for self-deception. We mask our true intentions by rationalizing what we do. The self-contradictoriness of a morally wrong maxim is indeed significant; but we have problems, first, with our ability (and willingness) to expose such contradictions and, second, with the limited extent of application that results. Common morality once again appears an inadequate source of moral knowledge.

Where then shall we turn? For the theist, the clue is the relationship of God to moral knowledge. We have, of course, the biblical revelation and the specific moral teaching it gives. We have drawn on what it says or implies about relativism, egoism and a purely consequentialist approach, about the good, about justice and love; we have its deontological emphasis on moral law. Now we must pick up on the biblical teaching about a general revelation of moral law accessible to all people at all times, to which all of us are accountable (Rom 1—3). I am not satisfied to locate that general revelation in a moral faculty or to give it an intuitionist interpretation.

Natural Law

The Bible comes closer, I suggest, to so-called natural law theories than it does to intuitionism. Here again care is needed, because natural law is sometimes identified with a common morality developed in the course of history. I have in mind, however, not this historicist view but instead the metaphysical natural law theories that find moral law written into the very nature of human existence.

The ancient Stoics initiated one such tradition.[9] All nature is governed by rational laws that keep it operating in harmonious and unified fashion, each part performing its proper function. Natural law is then what reason prescribes for the harmonious and just ordering of a society and, since we are rational beings, we can determine rationally what natural law requires. Centuries later, during the Enlightenment, this was picked up and further developed by John Locke, Thomas Jefferson and others in their theories of natural human rights divinely endowed. Locke also suggests that we can deduce moral law from the nature of the human person as a rational and self-determining being.[10] I shall return to this tradition when we discuss human rights in chapter nine.

Another tradition comes from Aristotle, who held that every kind of thing that exists is endowed by nature with an inherent end to which it tends. The essence of humanness is that of a rational animal, so our natural end, indeed our highest and all-encompassing end, is to live a life in accordance with reason.[11] Thomas Aquinas, the medieval Christian scholar, took this further: since God created us to pursue good ends, we should always seek the good and avoid evil. For all beings whose natural end is to exist, humans included, there is a natural law of self-preservation. We should, for instance, protect human life. Again, in common with other animals, we have an essential and natural sexual drive and a tendency to educate our offspring. This, too, is a good end to which natural law directs us. As distinctively rational beings, moreover, we are directed into a rationally ordered society and are intended to know the truth about God. So an orderly society and truth about God we should also pursue.[12]

Natural law theories have had a long and lasting influence in the history of ethics. Their attractiveness is evident in that they provide an objective, as against a subjective, basis for moral knowledge, and they check both common morality and individual beliefs by what is essential and universal to our humanness. The Stoic and Aristotelian versions, however, depend on their particular metaphysical theories, and no natural law ethic can be more firmly established than what it says about the *nature* of persons.

The Law of God and His Creation

The general concept of a moral law written into our nature as human beings is, however, theologically attractive.[13] This is an ordered creation, as we have observed before, and it is ordered with a view to God's purposes in creating as he did. What he created is good, and the ends for which he created are also good —good ends which we as God's servants should pursue. Equally telling, perhaps more so, are some biblical indications of this.

Paul in Romans 1 speaks of some human actions as contrary to nature: he echoes the Genesis record about man and woman created in God's image, their lives and their heterosexuality protected therefore by the law of creation (Gen 1:26-31; 2:18-25; 4:8-16; 9:1-6). Elsewhere, too, Scripture takes note of a creationally based morality (Mt 19:4-12; Mk 7:18-23; 1 Tim 4:1-5; Jas 3:9). The Old Testament prophets hold nations accountable that did not have access to the Jewish law. It would perhaps be too much to say that the creation *proves* each ingredient in God's moral law. The biblical direction is rather that the creation *bears witness* to the moral law, that creational indicators point to good ends God intended in making us as he did, and that God's law is the law of creation.

It is important here to distinguish what is *essential* to human nature, *inherent* in it, from what is culturally or historically relative, superimposed by a particular society or by individual differences. Some, like Jacques Ellul, have argued that human nature is not now as God intended, that our sinfulness has destroyed the original structure of things, or that Christ's kingdom is altogether new.[14] Theologians Thielicke and Bonhoeffer disagree, insisting that Jesus Christ himself is the Creator and that his grace restores us to the purposes for which he made us in the beginning (compare Heb 2:6-15).[15] The doctrine of common grace also assures us that God protects sinful people from the worst in themselves, bearing witness still to his creative wisdom and power.

But if disagreement about metaphysical views of human nature handicaps the older natural law theories, how can we proceed? Our starting points are the biblical indications that (1) this is an ordered creation and (2) we were made in God's image and for his purposes. To these we may add (3) the biblical recognition of universal spheres of human action such as those delineated in the second half of the Decalog, and (4) the divine appointment of some universal types of social institutions, such as those embodying the husband-wife relationship, economic relationships and the political order. These point out to us where natural moral indicators may be found in creation.

Parellels to this approach can be found in at least two philosophers. F. H. Bradley's famous essay "My Station and Its Duties" derives a knowledge of moral duties from what one's social, political or family status might be, for every role we play brings its own obligations. Bradley's problem was that his conception of a station in life was too largely that of the conservative Englishman of his day. Again, W. D. Ross speaks of "trailing obligations" that accompany various human relationships and activities.

Having made a promise, I have obligations. Being married and a parent brings obligations too. Both Bradley and Ross suggest in effect that we draw on a phenomenological description of universal aspects of human existence from which moral obligations follow.

A pattern for moral reasoning now emerges, suggested by the Christian doctrines of creation and general revelation but developed via an account of universal and essential features of human existence. With regard to any moral problem, several questions must be asked:

1. What universal human action spheres are involved (work, sex, play and so on), and what social institutions (family, government and so on)?

2. What are the essential purposes inherent in the nature of these human activities and these social institutions?

3. How can these purposes best be pursued with justice and love?

The first question is answered descriptively. But because each action sphere and institutional involvement brings its own moral responsibilities, we can speak with Ross of prima-facie duties.[16] When such duties conflict and moral dilemmas arise, then one's *actual* duty might be other than it would be in a simpler case. "Obey governmental authority" is a prima-facie rule to be consistently followed, and we need overriding moral justification for any exception. But exceptions arise, for instance, if we have to choose between disobeying government and surrendering our Jewish neighbors to the Gestapo, or if we are drafted to serve in an unjust and disproportionate war.

The second question, that of God's purposes inherent in our nature, may often be answered from a theology of our activities and institutions, a theology that draws together biblical indications about the purposes God intended in our sexuality, in our work and play, in the family, in government, and so forth. This requires a great deal of careful attention if we are to avoid slipping

into the fallacies and heresies of our day. But we may also tackle
the question on the basis of general revelation, from what we
know of the essential and unavoidably inherent nature of such
an activity or institution—despite our cultural or psychological
differences. Some understanding of pertinent sciences will help.
Are there features of human sexuality which speak to its intended
ends? or of human work? or of marriage and family? or of punishment?[17]

We must emphasize that in looking for biblical and natural
indications of the good ends we should pursue, we are, like
Aristotle, thinking of what is universal and essential to humans,
not what marks only some of us as individuals. Today's common
stress on self-actualization is individualistic, and a goal of individualistic self-actualization is a form of ethical egoism. Moreover, what promises to give us satisfaction and a sense of fulfillment individually may not at all be what God intended: our
individual possibilities may be distortions of what is good. For
the same reason, empirical generalizations about what people
find fulfilling are not enough. We must look for *creational* indicators of what is *inherent* and *essential*. In regard to sex, for
instance, potential for reproduction is biologically indisputable,
and this fact has moral implications we will pursue later.

The third question, about how we should pursue the good
ends for which we are created, presupposes a clear grasp of the
principles of justice and love and what they require, as well as
the ability to relate them to particulars. This is where consequences come in, for they affect the overall justice of an action
or policy; they will be agonized over with love. This stage is often
the hardest, for it requires a deep moral sensitivity, a careful
knowledge of all the factors involved and wisdom in putting it
all together. We must keep in mind that creationally based moral
knowledge, like knowledge of other sorts, is less explicit than
Scripture, and in acquiring it we are not infallible. Our ignorance
will show, as will our oversights, hasty judgments and lack of

wisdom. Our minds need always to be enlightened by God.

Observe where we have now come. Common morality, we argued, has some credibility but is piecemeal and subject to change. We needed both to account for its merits and to find something better grounded and more reliable. A creationally based ethic of the sort I have proposed is indeed better grounded, and the moral knowledge it affords is more self-critical and more reliable than unexamined intuitions or uncritical acceptance of a moral tradition. But at the same time it explains why common sense morality has the value it does, and why our moral intuitions should at least be considered. If the moral law is indeed written into the way we are made, if there are any natural moral indicators bearing witness to what God intended in essential and universal areas of human activity, then we should expect some degree of moral awareness to have developed in these regards. And that is what common morality often reveals. Some moral beliefs are indeed quite "natural."

Examples are now needed as to how the kind of moral knowledge envisioned here actually works, and these will follow shortly. But one further theoretical problem must come first: how can we move logically from what *is* essential and inherent in human existence to what *ought* to be? From where does the ought arise? The problem has haunted ethical theory, particularly the consequentialist views. How can a Christian ethic, which appeals to what *is,* handle the problem? That is the subject of our next chapter.

8

The Basis
of Obligation

*H*ow can we derive "ought" from "is"? How can empirical facts (or anything else that "is," for that matter) impose duties or obligations on us? Why, in a word, ought I be moral? Why be good?

Plato defined the good as the harmonious unity of all that is, and the moral good as a harmony of all the virtues under the rule of reason. Given this conception and its background in Plato's theory of eternal, impersonal forms as the model for all order and harmony, where does "ought" come in? Why ought we be good? What is there about Plato's forms that can bind us to our moral duty?

In his *Republic* Plato assumes that those who know what is good will love and desire it. But he also recognizes that moral virtue is itself a prerequisite to knowing the good. So I must both know the good in order to desire virtue, and be virtuous in order to know the good. In order to break into this vicious circle Plato proposes to organize society in such a way that those who do not know the good will be ruled by those who do. But the question remains, why *ought* those who know the good do it? They may *want* to, but *ought* they? Whence comes the obligation? Later, in his *Laws,* Plato excludes atheists from his ideal state, for since it is the gods who command our duties, the atheist will not be a good citizen. In the end, therefore, Plato seems to recognize the inadequacy of an impersonal, ideal good to create obligation.

Attractive as Plato has always been to Christian thinkers, here is one vast contrast. In Plato, the ultimate reality is an ideal that exists independently of any person, human or divine. In Christianity, the ultimate reality is a personal God. It is persons, not ideals, who command. Not surprisingly, this realization is echoed in modern ethical theories: duties arise in our relations to people. It is persons who impose obligations on us and hold us responsible, not natural consequences or metaphysical concepts as such.

This is one of the problems we noted in utilitarianism. However we may define the good, however well we may calculate consequences, to whatever extent we may or may not desire certain consequences, none of this of itself implies any obligation or command. That something *is* or will be does not imply that we *ought* to seek it. We can never derive an "ought" from a premised "is" unless the "ought" is somehow already contained in the premises.

English Catholic philosopher Elizabeth Anscombe suspects that since the utilitarianism of the first half of this century had no way of relating the ought to the good, it might as well have jettisoned the concepts of moral obligation and moral duty. They are just relics of the ethical conceptions of years gone by.[1]

When we ask who or what creates moral obligation, three alternatives arise. Obligation is self-imposed, imposed by people or imposed by God.

The Ought Is Self-Imposed

It is by my own act of will that I have any obligation at all. The French existentialist Jean Paul Sartre is explicit in this regard. In a universe in which God does not exist there has to be someone, he says, to invent values. A human being is nothing but what he makes of himself, so that we each bear the full responsibility for shaping our existence. But in choosing what we want to be, we "at the same time create an image of man as we think he *ought* to be."[2] This ought is entirely self-imposed.

Plainly Sartre's atheistic existentialism leaves no room for any higher authority than oneself. It echoes a loneliness in which each of us is an island—independent, self-governed, alienated from the rest of the world. It is a form of ethical subjectivism, for no objective moral order exists, neither Platonic forms nor natural law nor creation orders. The individual is autonomous. Freedom knows no bounds. Either I choose and then act on that choice, accepting the ought I have created, or else I lapse in bad faith into a valueless existence.

In Sartre the concept of human freedom has reached its zenith. Nurtured in the individualism of the Enlightenment, it found classic expression in Kant's emphasis on the autonomy rather than heteronomy of the will.[3] A heteronomous will is ruled by something other than oneself, by objects of desire or pressures of circumstance, and therefore it cannot act freely out of respect for duty. But an autonomous will is self-governed, as if reason laid down universal moral law without reference to any nonmoral interests. Kant's autonomous will acknowledged no higher authority than the universal demands of reason itself. But Sartre discards any notion of universal reason and moral law; he stretches the notion of autonomy to the extreme. I choose what I want independently, by myself, not under the rule of reason or law or anything else. My freedom is absolute.

Plainly such an extreme is fundamentally incompatible with the direction we have seen a Christian ethic taking. But the notion of a self-imposed ought has been developed in more moderate tones. Consider the notion of respect for persons—that we should, as Kant said, treat people not just as means but as ends of value in themselves. How does this obligation arise? One proposal begins with the fact that as a person I value myself in this way, and I expect from others the respect that will keep them from just using me. To be logically consistent, then, I ought to treat other persons as persons in the same way. The ought that arises is a *logical* one, needed to avoid self-contradiction in claiming that one person (that is, myself) should be treated as a person, yet other persons need not be.

The problem with this argument is that intrinsic value is assigned to persons (myself) from the beginning of the argument, and this begs the question. The argument begins with the purely descriptive statement that I value myself as a person. But ought I do so? What gives me the value I claim? What gives persons generally such value that it obligates others? If I simply claim it for myself, then the obligation is ultimately self-imposed, perhaps arbitrary. Indeed, the history of ethics has not always ascribed such value to persons, nor has human civilization. But if, instead of claiming it, I simply acknowledge a value and obligation that exist independently of whether or not I recognize it, then the basis of obligation is ultimately the Creator's will, not my own.

The Ought Is Socially Imposed

The most familiar version of this second alternative is undoubtedly a social contract theory, in which moral obligations arise in a civil society rather than in the state of nature. Living in such a society requires certain things of everybody. John Locke is our classic example: he speaks of marriage and family and government alike as contractual relationships, rather than as something inherent in the state of nature.[4]

More recent examples are plentiful. I have already mentioned F. H. Bradley's essay "My Station and Its Duties" and W. D.

Ross's "trailing obligations." To an extent, of course, they are correct that obligations do arise from our position in life and from our promises and other commitments. The point has been well made by J. R. Searle in his significantly titled essay "How to Derive Ought from Is."[5] An institution, he states, is a system of "constitutive rules": the institution of promising, for instance, necessarily has rules that obligate the parties involved. The ought follows from the very fact that such an institution as promising "is."

But, of course, this does not take care of the noninstitutionalized duties. And not every expectation constituted by an institution can be called good. For instance, a street gang might require at least one murder by every new member, and it might demand that one never "rat" on rival gangs. Neither the ends nor the means deemed essential to any institution are automatically good, and the social imposition of duties does not ipso facto make them morally right. Indeed, in some cases it might well be that one ought to do the opposite of what status or social expectation requires. If this is so, then apparently some other basis for obligation exists than the social imposition of duties.

Another similar example is John Rawls's attempt to base moral judgments on a hypothetical social agreement about justice as fairness. First, he says, each person is to have the greatest liberty compatible with similar greatest liberty for all. Second, social and economic inequalities are to be arranged for the greatest benefit of the least advantaged, while providing equal opportunity for all.[6] This ideal might well seem highly desirable, and our duties would rest on the rational choice of these principles. Yet what, other than enlightened self-interest, obligates us to be rational and to choose justice in the first place? This is no more than a hypothetical imperative: if we think justice as fairness is a good goal to seek, then we will accept the rules society imposes. Maybe we will, but the ought is still not unconditional.

I have been raising what Stephen Toulmin calls "limiting questions": why should we be concerned at all about social practices and moral expectations? R. M. Hare, who analyzes in detail the imperative or "commanding" function of moral language, raises the same point. Most theories, he argues, simply fail to account for the ought that commands us: subjectivism reduces imperatives to statements about subjective states, egoism and utilitarianism reduce them to statements about consequences, emotivism simply rejects them because they are not empirically verifiable, and determinism reduces them to causes rather than commands. The power of moral imperatives, he concludes, depends on my decision about the kind of person I want to be and the way of life I prefer.[7] That is the ultimate question. But so stated, duty turns out to be self-imposed after all, in his case a self-imposed utilitarian prescription.

Elizabeth Anscombe's point is well made. We have a problem introducing the ought into ethics unless, as she argues, we are morally obligated by law—not a socially imposed law, ultimately, but divine law. She continues:

> Naturally it is not possible to have such a conception unless you believe in God as a lawgiver. . . . But if such a conception is dominant for many centuries, and then is given up, it is a natural result that the concepts of obligation, of being bound or required by law, should remain though they had lost their root.[8]

This is precisely the problem with modern ethical theory in the West: it has lost its Judeo-Christian roots. It may even advocate virtues and practices that are in many instances compatible with a Christian ethic, but it has lost the binding force of divine commandments.

The Ought Is Divinely Imposed

We ought to do what God wills. This theme was obvious enough in the natural law theories we discussed earlier and which Anscombe had in mind. Why treat persons as ends and not just as means? Because God created the human person in his own image, thereby requiring a respect for persons that resembles respect for God. He is to be valued for himself, not just used as a means to my own self-interest. All people likewise, for they are in God's image; as we put it in our last chapter, universal aspects of human existence bear witness to what God wills. Even more explicit about the divine basis of obligation are the divine command theories which have arisen throughout the history of ethics.[9]

The Bible is quite clear about our obligation to God's commandments. They guided human life from the beginning of creation (Gen 1:27-30; 2:15-17). They were spelled out more fully in the Mosaic law, reiterated throughout the Old Testament and restated in the New (Mt 5:17-20; Jn 15:12-17; 1 Jn 2:1-6 and so on). John Calvin enumerated three functions of God's law: to expose our sin and point us to God's mercy in Jesus Christ, to restrain evildoing by fear of its penalties, and to instruct us in the ways of righteousness. In a word, God imposes the ought.

The outcome is not the autonomous will which Kant affirmed, imposing moral obligation on itself—unless we do so by heartily accepting our overriding obligation to God. Nor is it the heteronomous will Kant rejected, which is swayed all the time by nonmoral or immoral things. It is rather a "theonomous" will, bowing to the higher authority of God.[10] Some have objected that this means we abdicate all responsibility for our actions, like the Nazi SS trooper blindly obeying orders. On the contrary, when we are commanded to love God, to love our fellows, to love God's law, this is not the unthinking and uncaring conformity of a puppet but the heartfelt and deliberate obedience of a morally responsible person.

A theonomous ethic leaves open the question of moral knowledge. Some writers treat divine command theories as theories about moral knowledge, implying that we are confined to what the Bible says or to special experiences of divine guidance. Not so. In the last chapter we saw other ways of knowing made possible by a general revelation in moral matters. In any case, the Bible does not answer all our ethical questions, nor does it automatically resolve moral dilemmas. Many things remain for us to work through, not least the agonizing moral decisions which the technology and complexity of today's world require. Divine command theories speak rather to the *basis* of moral obligation than to questions of moral knowledge. The fact that God's will is made known through things he *made* as well as things he *said* does not make his will any less a command.

But does this really avoid the is/ought problem that haunts ethical theory? Does the *fact* that God wills something really imply that we ought to do it? Factual premises alone do not imply moral duties, it is true, but "*God* wills it" is *not only* a factual statement. It is loaded with all that the name *God* entails, and in theistic language *God* is already a morally significant term. We are speaking of the Creator and Lord of the universe, who as such commands final authority over every creature. We are speaking of the God of perfect love and perfect justice, who by his very nature sets all moral standards for others. We are speaking of God the Redeemer, to whom we owe grateful loyalty. If God is all this, then indeed the ought follows from the is. In the words of the Westminster Shorter Catechism, "because God is the Lord, and our God and Redeemer, therefore we are bound to keep all his commandments."

In his *Euthyphro,* Plato asked whether the gods command something because it is right or whether it is right because they command it. Plato's philosophy implied that moral ideals, like other forms, exist independently, guiding both men and gods. But medieval Christian theologians found that unacceptable. Some of them argued that God's commandments are what they are because he freely and sovereignly willed them thus (a position known as voluntarism). But could God have made stealing and lying right, had he so chosen? Do God's commands really make morality that arbitrary? Could God as well have commanded us to torture innocent children with relentless cruelty? Plainly not, for we are not speaking of either a sadistic or an amoral deity, but of a God who is just and loving, both Creator and Redeemer, who by virtue of his own character would do no such thing.

God's will cannot be separated from his nature. He wills what he does because he is the God he is. What he wills for us invariably relates to his own justice and love, and to his good purposes in creation and redemption. It will therefore, in the final analysis, be the most just and loving thing we can do.

But what of those who believe no such God exists? Are they then freed from all moral obligation? Indeed not. For it is *facts* about God, not our belief or unbelief, that implies the ought. The apostle Paul makes that plain enough in Romans 1—2: even those who refuse "to retain God in their knowledge" are still morally accountable (1:28 KJV).

Some prophets of moral gloom declare that without Christian belief no morality even resembling this is possible, and that our society thus faces moral disaster, even anarchy. Two responses are possible. First, where no divinely imposed ought is acknowledged, other bases of obligation are created. The ought is either socially imposed or self-imposed (and these become pseudo-religious bases, as in Marxism or secular humanism), or else some non-Christian religion takes over this role. These bases may be philosophically insufficient, as we have argued regarding the first two alternatives, and theologically objectionable to Christians. But neither of these considerations forces people to abandon all sense of ought. The irony is that the merciful providence of God makes even mistaken views of ethical obligation serve some of his moral ends. Moral anarchy does not necessarily result from nontheistic belief, though logically it might.

This realization leads to a second response to the prophet of gloom. There are other connections between religion and true morality than the logical one we have been exploring. Obviously there is a historical connection in that Western morality (and, to a much lesser extent, non-Western) has been powerfully influenced in the past by the pervasiveness of the Judeo-Christian heritage. Social institutions and legal systems are influenced by it, not to mention non-Christian ethicists themselves, and the causal influence continues in the lingering notion of moral duty. Further, there is a psychological connection between religion and morality such that even nominal theists have a sense of ought that reflects the expectations of a law of God. Again, there is an epistemological connection, for if the law of God is attested by essential structures of human nature, by our common needs and spheres of action, then these factors are likely to influence the ethical thinking and moral decisions even of those who do not acknowledge the Creator. If God's laws are indeed beneficial, then people are somewhat likely to recognize it, whether or not they recognize the lawgiver. Of course, as Paul notes in Romans 1, God may give them up to their own passions. Yet even then he does not leave them alone: government has its divinely ordained functions in this regard, as do the family and the economic order. God has many ways of preserving us from evil. Some of these will surface as we discuss some moral issues of today.

At this point we complete our discussion of ethical theory. Our proposals have included (1) a structure for Christian ethics that distinguishes cases, area rules, the overall principles of justice and love, and their logical basis, (2) an approach to moral knowledge via biblical and natural indicators of God's purposes for us in his creation, and (3) the basis of our obligation in the divine nature and will. In discussing emotivist and consequentialist theories, we asked what moral terms like *good* and *right* mean. To what do they refer? Moral judgments, we argued, are interpretive or evaluative statements. Now it can also be said that they interpret actions and policies in the light of God's will, and that moral language therefore refers ultimately to God's love and justice in relation to what he purposes for his creation. Where this takes us in practice we shall now begin to see.

9

Human
Rights

S ince World War 2, problems
about human rights have repeatedly claimed public attention.
They arose first in regard to the Nazis, then concerning equal
access by black people to education, employment, voter registra-
tion and the use of public facilities, then over the rights of women
and other minorities, and most recently in United States foreign
policy. Racial and sexual discrimination is a continuing concern,
and we have belatedly gained sensitivity to abuses of the poor
and the repression of political opposition. Meanwhile, debates
about the right to life, the right to privacy, the rights of criminals
and property rights demand thoughtful moral decisions.

The Doctrine of Human Rights
In asserting any human right, the underlying claim is that all persons have an equal right to be treated as persons—regardless of
differences in race, religion, sex, politics, or social and economic

status.[1] Such differences are ethically irrelevant and do not affect the essential nature and worth of a person. Discrimination, however, makes such differences count; it treats people unequally by virtue of race or sex or some other irrelevant factor. To pay women less than men for the same work, simply because they are women, is discrimination. To provide black people with inferior education and job opportunities to those provided for whites is discrimination. To prevent the poor from voting, simply because they are poor or because they resent the establishment, is discrimination. And discrimination violates human rights.

It is important here to distinguish *human* rights (sometimes called natural rights) from the *special* rights that arise from a legal contract, a constitution, a particular relationship (like that of husband and wife or parent and child) or even an informal promise. Legal and constitutional rights and other special rights are not universal, but apply only to those who fulfill certain special conditions, such as signing a contract, being a citizen or having a child. Special rights do not apply to persons considered simply as persons, members of the human community at large, but they are granted to those who fulfill special conditions: they are in that sense conditional, not unconditional, rights. But human rights apply to all persons simply as persons. They are then universal rights, inherent rights, equal rights. They are unconditional.

This does not mean that one should always claim those rights or exercise them. Indeed, by "turning the other cheek" I may decline to assert my rights. Nor can we invariably allow others the free exercise of theirs. A young child under the care and authority of parents or guardians does not exercise fully all the freedoms his rights imply; and criminal punishment keeps the convicted offender from exercising one or more of his rights. But we have a prima-facie obligation to allow all people the free exercise of their rights, and exceptions to the obligation are subject to morally overriding conditions. Young children are still to be respected as persons with human rights: although they do not now exercise all their rights themselves, others may assert those rights on their behalf. Nor are all of a convicted criminal's rights taken away from him while he is incarcerated. He remains a person and, as we shall see in chapter ten, his personhood is still to be respected even while he is being punished. In this sense human rights are unalienable, for persons always remain persons and are to be treated as such.

If we admit that we all equally have the right to be treated as persons, then it follows that we have the duty to respect one another accordingly. Rights bring correlative duties: my rights to life and liberty imply that you ought to respect these rights. Of course, not all duties arise in response to human rights. Some issue from special relationships, like contracts and the special rights they involve; and some duties come from loving and caring for another person rather than from that person's rights.

The Significance of Human Rights

The value of this human rights doctrine can hardly be over-estimated. In the first place, it provides a vehicle for understanding and unpacking the related ideas of liberty and justice. To have a right to something means that one should, apart from overriding moral considerations, have the liberty to exercise that right. Rights and liberties intertwine. Human rights relate to those liberties which are essential to a human quality of existence, just as special rights protect those which are essential to a special relationship. Justice, defined in shorthand terms as "treating equals equally," means respecting and preserving equally the rights of all.

In the second place, human rights are basic to more particular rights. A woman's rights as a human person, equal to those of a man, undergird her rights as wife or employee. Because she is a person with full human rights, promises to her must be as fully kept as promises to anyone else. Likewise an employee's rights

may be set forth in a contract, but she has as much right as the
president of the company to have contract rights respected.

Similarly, in politics, the United States' Declaration of Independence asserts that governments are instituted to secure our
natural rights, and the French Constitution of 1791 states that
the end of all political association is the preservation of these
rights. This means, on the one hand, that natural rights are not
just legal rights given us by the state or by a constitution. Like
the ought discussed in the last chapter, they are ultimately neither
self-imposed nor socially imposed. On the other hand, it means
that government is not the master but a servant of the people in
the exercise of their natural rights.

Third, the value of the concept of human rights is that it avoids
ethical egoism even while it emphasizes the value of the individual. Egoism, as we saw in chapter four, can engender an
extreme individualism which disregards responsibilities to other
persons. But rights are not whatever we *want*. The utilitarian
Jeremy Bentham, in an essay called "Anarchical Fallacies," com-
plained that the assertion of natural rights incites "selfish and
dissocial passions," the great enemies of public peace, and so mili-
tates against social order and the laws of the land. He failed to
see that the built-in balancing of equal individual rights tips
things in the very opposite direction. The human rights doctrine,
by insisting on the *equal* rights of *all* persons, disallows "me-
first" extremes. My individual rights can neither exclude nor take
precedence over others' rights, for they stand or fall together.
And, because rights imply obligations, we are morally bound
together in a mutually supportive society.

In similar fashion, the theory of human rights avoids the pit-
falls of cultural relativism, for rights are universal and unchanging. That is not an empirical description of the political or legal
status quo, of course, but rather a normative statement of what
ought to be. So the relativist's empirical diversity thesis discussed
in chapter two is irrelevant as a criticism of human rights theory.

And since human rights exist independently of social or political conditions, his dependency thesis also is beside the point. Those theses pertain to de facto situations, not to an ideal rooted in the universal nature and worth of persons.

What I have said of human rights vis-à-vis egoism and relativism can be extended to utilitarianism too. Jeremy Bentham could make no sense of the claim that all people *possess* equal rights, for empirically the exercise of rights must be protected by an established government.[2] And Mill based his idea of justice on the utility principle, so that we grant rights for the benefit of society rather than their being in some sense inherent in individual persons.[3] The utilitarian thus tends to regard human rights as humanly (that is, socially or legally) conferred, in effect eliminating the difference between natural and special rights. But if human rights exist only for utilitarian ends, might they not also be suspended or even denied altogether if greater utility were thereby served? And then we must ask again what remains to protect a minority or an innocent party, or to maintain the equal treatment of equals. People are not faceless placeholders in a utility calculus, but individual persons, each of value in his or her own right.

The concept of the equal worth and equal rights of all persons is deeply rooted in the biblical picture of society and government. Again and again the Scriptures affirm the value God places on the human individual: even the hairs of his head are numbered. The Old Testament prophets hold rulers accountable for a justice that respects the rights of the poor and fatherless, and they picture a coming kingdom of peace, economic sufficiency and social justice for all. And recall how Jesus treated the Samaritan woman (a Samaritan and a woman!) and the little children. God is "no respecter of persons," no chauvinist or racist or otherwise a discriminator.

The human rights concept was developed in Roman jurisprudence, especially in the writings of Cicero, and in the Stoic idea of a universal human citizenship. But the Enlightenment in Britain, France and Germany formulated it in modern terms, perhaps most notably English philosopher John Locke in his *Second Treatise on Civil Government*. It was on these sources that the founding fathers of the United States drew when they asserted that all men are endowed by their Creator with certain unalienable rights. Human rights were later reaffirmed and extended in the Universal Declaration of Human Rights adopted in 1948 by the United Nations. Properly understood, however, it is a concept whose inspiration is thoroughly theistic and Christian.

The Basis for Human Rights

It is one thing to assert human rights and to prefer this doctrine to those of the egoist, relativist or utilitarian. But on what basis can we assert it? How can people "possess" rights that a society and its laws may not recognize? How can rights "inhere" naturally in a person?

The peculiarity of the language is indeed perplexing. A. I. Melden in his book *Rights and Persons* gives perhaps the best recent explanation. Melden roots rights in relationships between persons considered as moral agents. As members of the human community, a community of moral agents all pursuing their own interests, we accord to others the same right to pursue their interests as we ask for ourselves. The paradigm case is that of a promise: promising is a rights-granting activity, and the recognition of other persons as moral agents is like promising to respect their right to pursue their own ends. In this sense human relations are rights-granting activities, too, and human rights are logical corollaries of belonging to the human community. They are *inherent* in life together.

So far so good. But do we not have here another version of what in the last chapter we called a socially imposed ought? What of the person who refuses to live as a participant in the human community, or who simply refuses to play by the rules? Does he not have human rights? What value has a hermit except to himself? And is the harmony of a rights-giving human community any more than a matter of utility? Does Melden really tell us what gives a human person the value we say that person now "possesses"?

The words "endowed by their Creator with unalienable Rights" are significant. Rights are not socially accorded but God-given. They may be essential to a human community of moral agents, but it is God who in the first place made us responsible agents to live together in community. What then does it mean to say that rights are God-given?

Let us go back to the underlying assumption of the value and dignity of persons and ask how we account for that. Does it arise only from our value to ourselves and other people? Or does it not refer more fundamentally to our value to God and to his purpose for us in creation? A person is more than a demographic statistic, more than a body plus a flux of experience, more even than an economic and political being and a member of those communities. Created by God in God's own image, human persons mirror God himself, our personhood reflecting the nature of God, our individuality and relationships and activities finitely imaging God's character, relationships and activities. God values us as his own creatures (for all creation bears witness), but also as persons (for he too is Person). To treat a person as a person, to respect her rights as a person, therefore respects both God's handiwork and God himself. To abuse a person, to violate her rights, is to disrespect God and depreciate his image in her. It is in effect an act of blasphemy, for the sanctity of persons reflects the sanctity of God.[4]

But we can go further than this. To image God in his creation is to be a caring steward of our environment and a responsible agent in every sphere of activity. Human rights are in effect the right to fulfill our God-given calling freely, without obstruction by others. The right to be treated as a person is then the right to the responsible life God has purposed for us.

A Christian understanding of human rights thus goes beyond the Enlightenment understandings incorporated into a democratic political heritage. A right is a license, not to psychological or ethical egoism, not to the exaltation or exaggeration of our liberties, but for personal development through a life of freely given service. Sometimes the conscientious and humble believer, faced with *his* rights, maintains that a Christian has no rights of his own but has given them all up to Christ. This may be an unwitting depreciation of the dignity and value of God's image in us. What he really means, I suggest, is that he does not insist on justice for himself all the time but is prepared to turn the other cheek and go a second mile out of love. He means that by God's grace he has the right and privilege of freely serving others. Rights are not ends in themselves to be selfishly and tenaciously grasped (recall Jesus' own example), but are means to manifesting God's image more freely. They are to be viewed, like everything else, in theocentric rather than egocentric fashion.

The Extent of Human Rights

Human rights boil down essentially to the right to be treated as a person. But what does this include? What rights are *human* rights, and how can we identify them?

The clue is to know what is essential to being a human person. John Locke listed three natural rights, and we can start with these: life, liberty and property. Each of these he saw as essential to personal existence. The right to life obviously is prerequisite to all else. The right to liberty respects the self-determination of one endowed with the capacity for deliberation and free choice. The right to property is concerned that the fruit of one's labor should meet basic needs and sustain a human quality of life. God has endowed us with these in making us the human persons we are. But in each case the right in question is limited by the rights of others, for we have the duty to respect others' lives, others' liberty, others' property. They equally are human persons, and theirs are *equal* human rights.

Might other human rights be added to this list? The right to pursue happiness was included in the American Declaration of Independence, but this depends on how we define *happiness*. If we equate it simply with pleasure or enjoyment, giving it hedonistic overtones, then we misunderstand the intention. Happiness, in the classical sense, is simply "well-being," the satisfaction not only of economic needs, as suggested by Locke's "right to property," but also of psychological and other genuinely human needs. It suggests a markedly human quality of life. On this basis we might include the right to whatever is necessary "for life and godliness": freedom of information, freedom of association, freedom of religion and so forth. On this basis, too, we must object to abuses of human rights, whether in Soviet Russia, Latin America or the United States.

Some problem areas now begin to surface. On these we can here make only a few comments to illustrate how the human rights doctrine works. Consider property rights a little further. Aristotle distinguished between natural and unnatural money getting, where the latter goes beyond providing a human quality of life to excessive luxury and self-indulgence. Aquinas maintained that property must be used for the benefit of others, and Locke reminded us that God gave the resources of creation to all people equally and for the benefit of all. The concern throughout is to avoid both absolute (that is, unlimited) wealth and absolute (that is, unalleviated) poverty. To that end our work and property are to serve others as well as ourselves.

In the Old Testament, travelers and the poor were free to glean grain from others' fields, and the Jubilee Year provided a periodic return of sold or mortgaged property to the original families—thereby preventing the perpetuation of hopeless destitution. The medievals for similar reasons objected to usury, and John Locke told settlers in the New World to leave enough land for others. In our own day we speak of fair wages, fringe benefits and the personal satisfactions that work should afford. But work, like money and property, is not only and not primarily for personal profit. It should both meet our own needs and be a vehicle for serving others. No *unlimited* property rights exist.

Consider women's rights. If we take human rights seriously at all, then women and men are equally persons and have equal human rights. This fact should be recognized and protected legally: equal pay for equal work, equal opportunity, equal legal status. It also provides the basis for genuinely egalitarian marriage, whatever the arrangement of roles a couple may choose. The problem that can arise, however, is that rights are sometimes stretched to egoistical extremes and may be confused with wants. Individual fulfillment, enjoyment and career plans then take precedence over everything else. But marriage is not a contract between two individuals, each with separate goals and plans; it is a union of two lives, shared values and common goals, their separate interests continuing partly merged and partly waived for the other's sake and their common good. In marriage, as in many other relationships, individual interests exist in a context of service to others.

Consider the abortion debate in this light, where one (and only one) of the issues involved pits the right to privacy against the fetus's right to life. This sounds like a classic case of conflicting obligations, both of which cannot be fulfilled at the same time. Let us then look a little more closely.

First, what about the claim that a fetus has the right to life? The Old Testament plainly values fetal life as a distinctive work of God rather than treating is as another "piece of tissue" (Eccles 11:5; Ps 139:13-16; Jer 1:5). Biologically, too, any human fetus is of course human life; and, even though it is not yet an *actual person* in the sense of a self-conscious and reflective being relating meaningfully to others, it is a *potential person* likely to develop all the powers adults have. As such its life is to be received and protected as a gift from God. Abortion on demand, for personal convenience or as a regular means of birth control, fails to recognize this. But that is not to say that an early fetus as a *potential* person shares full human rights equally with *actual* persons. The justice issue here is not the same as with murder or genocide. So while a prima-facie rule against abortion is morally requisite, possible exceptions may justly be considered when other moral obligations conflict with this one.

If the fetal life threatens the mother's right to life, most people would allow an abortion. I suggest this is because actual personhood has greater value than potential personhood: the mother's right to life ranks higher. But what about the mother's right to privacy, the freedom and privacy of her own body? Does that right override the sanctity of fetal life? If the right to privacy has been violated against the mother's will, as in the case of rape victims, then we might have reason to consider an abortion. But if the mother has voluntarily waived that right in sexual intercourse, knowing the possible outcome, then it would seem self-contradictory to talk of a violation of the right to bodily privacy. In such instances that right can hardly count more than fetal life, unless there are further significant moral considerations.

In the final analysis, questions of rights are also questions of responsibilities. Responsibility for one's sexual behavior and its consequences implies responsibility for the fetus, increasingly so as it advances toward actual personhood. Sometimes, too, self-giving love will go a second mile out of concern for the child-to-be.

Human rights are a matter of justice, then. But love as well as justice must be our concern. Love will seek justice and concern itself with others' rights. But love will also go the second mile, deferring and even waiving some rights at times in loving service to others. Marriage and parenthood require this of both partners, and they can teach us how to combine justice with love in other areas too.

10

Criminal Punishment

T he morality of punishment poses a number of important issues. In the first place, it addresses one of the major social problems of our day, one that resists solution but has been a major concern to Christians throughout history. In the second place, it provides a clear example of ethical theories at work and illustrates both their strengths and their weaknesses. Finally, the morality of punishment raises questions about human rights, for punishment suspends the free exercise of one's right to liberty or property, and capital punishment abrogates the right to life itself.[1]

Christian concern about punishment cannot be overstressed. The theme, not only of divine punishment of human sin but also of criminal punishment by civil authorities, pervades the Old Testament. The Mosaic law included a detailed penal code, and prophets like Habakkuk were quick to expose the failure of criminal justice. Yet Scripture also speaks of mercy for the sinner, and

Jesus Christ enjoins our care for prisoners when he says that what
we do for them we do also for him (Mt 25:31-46). We do well not
to forget this in the exercise of criminal justice.

The Utilitarian View

Jeremy Bentham launched the utilitarian ethic into its modern
orbit with proposals about punishment. In *An Introduction to the
Principles of Morality and Legislation,* he contended that we can
change human conduct by controlling the amounts of pleasure
and pain people experience. By imposing enough pain to outweigh the pleasure associated with a crime, we can effectively
deter would-be criminals from criminal behavior; and, as penolo-
gists today stress, the certainty and propinquity of pain are necessary to an effective deterrent. Subsequent utilitarian approaches
have emphasized not only deterrence but also rehabilitation and
the protection of society as the ends which punishment should
serve.

The attraction of this view lies not only in its concern for
society but also in its benevolent attitude toward the offender.
It is vastly better to rehabilitate than simply to incarcerate, better
for both society and the criminal. In addition, Bentham's proposal should be read against the background of the gallows used
in his day far too readily for far too many kinds of crime. He
wanted genuinely humanitarian reform.

In the course of time, however, serious questions have arisen
about the effectiveness of punishment for either deterrence or
rehabilitation. The recidivism rate in this country remains high,
and no clear evidence exists that even capital punishment deters.
The problem lies at least partially in the complexity and cost of
designing and operating an ideally utilitarian penal system. This
raises questions about people and why they act as they do. Here
the shortcomings of utilitarianism show up. Bentham assumed
the truth of psychological hedonism, an account of human behavior which, like psychological egoism, is at least incomplete.

He believed that we can calculate accurately the pleasure and pain resulting from a crime and its punishment. He supposed that a wrongdoer calculates such consequences before he acts, rather than behaving spontaneously or compulsively. Here are what in chapter five we labeled the problems of defining the good and of calculating consequences.

From an ethical standpoint, however, the problem of distributive justice, that is, the problem of treating people fairly and equitably, is even more acute. Two persons, let us suppose, commit identical crimes. Yet one gets far more pleasure from it than the other, and so will need more pain in punishment in order to be deterred from further violations. But is it just to punish one more than the other if the crimes are identical?

Or let us suppose that one has twice as high a pain threshold as the other. Should she then receive twice the punishment received by the other? And if a little surplus pain deters a little, perhaps a lot of surplus pain will deter more firmly still. The more punishment, the better? How does a utilitarian know when enough is enough and more would be counterproductive, except by experimenting? But experimenting on people? Most seriously of all, why should deterrence be limited to the guilty? If prevention is better than cure, why not make the innocent sample what is coming to them if they misbehave?

This sounds bizarre. Yet if the utility principle prevails, and if justice is simply a distributive arrangement which maximizes social good, then what moral protection do either the guilty or innocent really have? Like Pontius Pilate we might find it more beneficial to condemn the innocent than to acquit them (Lk 23:13-25). And what moral safeguards protect the guilty from inequitable sentencing? They might receive punishment grossly disproportionate to the crime. In effect, innocent and guilty persons alike could be used as means to the greatest benefit for the greatest number of people, rather than be treated as persons in their own right. The problem of distributive justice persists.

Another utilitarian approach backs away from talk of deterrence and equal justice altogether. British sociologist Barbara Wootton tries to erase the distinction between penal and medical institutions by doing away with the idea of punishment and replacing it with psychological and social therapy.[2] Once again this is well intentioned and compassionate, for criminal behavior is undoubtedly affected by emotional factors and social conditions, and some offenders may be suffering from severe mental illness or social alienation.

These problems certainly need attention. But the substitution of therapy for all punishment across the board is highly objectionable. First, it assumes that offensive behavior is determined entirely by conditions completely beyond the person's control, that the offender could not possibly have been a law-abiding citizen. Second, it depersonalizes the offender by denying him any moral responsibility for his own behavior. Third, it manipulates those who violate society's norms so as to make them conform willy-nilly. But who is to determine the ends of such therapy? Whose norms will be imposed? What might have happened to Martin Luther King, Jr., at the hands of radically racist therapists? Or to Jesus Christ at the hands of self-righteous establishment therapists? Shades of Huxley's *Brave New World* and Orwell's *1984* arise, worlds that stifle nonconformity and reform by means of genetic manipulation, behavior modification and thought control. Where does the therapeutic approach stop, once an authority takes charge and treats individuals as amoral means to establishment ends? Plainly controls are needed to protect human rights and to prevent the dehumanization of those who deviate.

The Retributivist View

A person is morally accountable for his actions, and guilt merits appropriate punishment: these together form the retributivist's thesis. Unfortunately retribution is too often caricatured or ill conceived as revenge and retaliation, intentions which Scripture, while endorsing punishment, plainly disavows (Rom 12:17—13:5). Law-abiding conduct is instead made a matter of conscience, a personal moral responsibility (Rom 13:5).

Let us look more closely. The legal concept of *mens rea* means that to be accountable one must be "of a right mind." To hold someone accountable is to treat him as a human person who knew what he was doing, who was free either to do it or not. In this sense, the right to be treated as a person, the right to be held accountable, is also the *right* to be punished.[3]

But the retributivist goes further than that. He also holds the corollary of that right—namely, that society has a *duty* to punish criminal offenders. Biblically, I think this, too, is clear: "the sword" is entrusted by God to government for the maintenance of peace and justice, and this mandate includes criminal punishment (Rom 13:4; 1 Pet 2:13-14). In the Old Testament, punishment meant restitution rather than revenge, plus a kind of negative wage. The thief was ordered to restore four- or fivefold to his victim, not just to return the stolen goods but also to pay a severe penalty. Of course, in some cases actual restitution is not possible—a life cannot be restored, for example—but then punishment becomes a symbolic restitution instead, as if it were paying one's debt to society. The concern is for victims as well as offenders, for both are human persons with rights of their own. In a similar vein, Aristotle speaks of "rectificatory" justice, rectifying the ill by restoring a just distribution. Retributive justice is then an application of the distributive justice which government has a duty to uphold.

One further element is essential to the retributivist approach, and it is summed up in the Old Testament *lex talionis*, "eye for eye, tooth for tooth" (Lev 24:20). This, too, has nothing to do with revenge, but is rather a limiting principle. The ancient Near East went to ghastly excesses of punishment. (And not long ago pickpockets were hanged in England, while in America a black person could be lynched without trial for less than a capital offense.) The *lex talionis* was a just and humanitarian measure, limiting punishment to what is proportionate to the crime: not a *head* for an eye, but simply an eye for an eye. Just punishment is restitution, then, plus a negative wage, but all in proportion to the offense.

A Combined View

Does moral concern about punishment stop here? I think not. Two universal moral principles must operate in this and every area of life: not only justice, but also love. A Christian ethic will be concerned about the consequences of punishment, concerned for what it does to the criminal, concerned for him as one created in God's image, one whom God loves and for whom Christ died. This ethic leads further to efforts at rehabilitation and, in a very broad sense, the redemption of a life.

The outcome is a combination of retributivist and utilitarian emphases.[4] Retributivism's strength lies in its emphasis on persons as morally responsible agents, on the duty of government to punish justly, and on limited and proportionate means. The strength of the utilitarian approach is its concern for a good outcome. Distinguish, however, rehabilitation *as* or *instead of* punishment from rehabilitative experiences *while* being punished. Utilitarians fail to make this distinction. They would justify punishment in general and award particular sentences on the basis of what punishment (or therapy) itself might achieve. But the combination I propose justifies and awards punishment on a retributivist basis, and then goes a second mile in providing rehabilitative experiences *while* the offender is being punished— experiences such as job training and work-release programs, psychological counseling, educational opportunity, religious activity, social service, supervised parole.

What should be done, for instance, with a first offender suspected of stealing? The retributivist will insist that he be held accountable, that the case be brought to trial, and that a fair sentence be given. Law and order must be firmly enforced. The utilitarian will want rather to nip criminal behavior in the bud and would perhaps consider counseling and probation, or required social service, rather than incarceration with habitual felons. An advocate of the combined view finds merit in both approaches, insisting that rehabilitation must not replace punishment, nor punishment preclude rehabilitation. He will therefore want to separate first offenders from hardened criminals and make provision for work-release and supervised probation without minimizing the accountability of the offender or the seriousness of the offense. Punishment there must be, but society also has a responsibility to help the offender avoid repeating his mistake.

Immense difficulties confront the application of such ideals to existing penal institutions and impede movement toward penal reform. Simply the complexities of collecting and enforcing restitution payments can obstruct progress along that avenue. But one area of application demands special ethical attention—namely, capital punishment.

We cannot argue biblically against all capital punishment *on principle,* for the "sword" was entrusted to government, and the Mosaic system allowed capital punishment for at least ten different crimes—crimes of violence, sex and lawlessness. But by the same token we cannot argue from biblical precedent *for* capital punishment as it is currently practiced, because biblical precedent granted the death penalty not only for murder but also for adultery or for cursing one's parents. We remember Jesus' treatment of the woman apprehended in the act of adultery (Jn 8:3-11). We can also not simply say that antiquity had no alternative forms of punishment; in addition to actual restitution, the Mosaic code provided for flogging and exile.

How then does the precedent help us? First, capital punishment is in principle a morally permissible option. Second, the *lex talionis* limits its use to the most extreme of crimes. Why then was it extended to those ten offenses? Not, according to the modified retributivist view I have developed, for utilitarian reasons. In any case, no clear evidence exists that the threat of capital punishment effectively deters. Instead, biblical history exhibits a developmental pattern in its handling of social evils and abuses of authority.

Take slavery: The Mosaic law allowed slavery but protected slaves from physical abuse and provided for periodic release. The prophets held society accountable to the law, while preaching mercy, justice and freedom from oppression. The gospel brings love, the underlying spirit of the law, more fully into view, so that Paul could tell Philemon to receive his runaway slave back as a Christian brother. Finally, the kingdom that is yet fully to come is announced as one with perfect justice for all, a kingdom with slavery gone forever. A similar pattern may be traced in the biblical treatment of divorce, war and other moral tragedies in human affairs: law, prophet and gospel together work at restraining evil and creating a hunger and thirst for righteousness that Christ's kingdom will eventually fill.

So, too, regarding capital punishment. In extreme cases it may be morally permissible—but it is not morally ideal. The *lex talionis* permits punishment proportionate to taking a person's life; but one may forfeit the right to live his own life by other means than death, and love will always seek the more redemptive alternative. Then, too, in our present legal system with all its practical inequities for minorities and for the poor, for example, equal access to legal resources still eludes many. We must wonder therefore whether capital punishment today is just. Justice we must always seek, but a justice tempered by love.

Can We Legislate Morality?

*B*oth of the questions we have so far raised in applied ethics have to do with the relation of law to morality. Human rights provide both an ethical basis for government and moral limitations on its power. Punishment, within moral limits, is part of government's responsibility for justice. Now we turn to a further question in this area: can we legislate specific moral matters? If so, how far can this extend?

Today the question is posed by the Moral Majority's advocacy of a variety of moral concerns, and not least by the right-to-life movement. Yet it is an age-old question. In Old Testament Israel, the civil and criminal laws spoke to most matters in the moral law, so that sexual deviancy was treated as a criminal offense along with murder. One exception was the sin of coveting, something hardly overt enough to be proven legally, at least until it issues in illegal action. But otherwise crimes and sinful acts were not distinguished. Calvin's Geneva and Hawthorne's Puritan New England also treated immoral behaviors as criminal offenses, for they were, like Israel, theocratic societies which accepted the governance of God over all areas of life.

A similar spirit inspired social-reform crusades like the British antislavery movement led by William Wilberforce, and the American abolitionist and prohibitionist movements. One anti-slavery leader in the 1830s declared, "A perfect state of society is . . . where what is right in theory exists in fact, where practice coincides with principle, and the law of God is the law of the land."[1]

This equation of sin and crime may well make sense for a con-fessedly theocratic society where an overwhelming moral con-sensus exists. But it poses serious problems for human rights and individual liberties in pluralistic contexts, like twentieth-century America or modern Israel. Even worse consequences are evident in the Ayatollah Khomeini's Iran, which utterly disre-gards the rights of dissenting minorities. If morality is to be legally enforced, whose morality will it be? Christians may per-haps welcome the enforcement of a Christian morality, but would they welcome the enforcement of other values that conflict with their own—let us say, laws requiring euthanasia for all persons seventy or over to make room for the children which every woman legally must bear, whether married or not? Then, too, in practical terms, how can we effectively enforce private moral behavior?

A classic case arose in the 1950s over the Wolfenden report in England.[2] A commission had been appointed to reconsider exist-ing criminal sanctions against homosexuality and prostitution, and it recommended the decriminalization of homosexual be-havior between consenting adults in private. In drawing the line between private behavior and matters of public decency, it drew on John Stuart Mill's libertarian view that society may only restrict individual freedoms in order to prevent harm to others.[3] Since private and voluntary homosexual activity harms no others, it was argued, the law cannot forbid it. Indeed, intrusions on privacy would cause more harm and offense than would allowing it to go on.

In contrast to the libertarian, the legal moralist wants laws forbidding immoral behavior primarily because it is immoral. The paternalist, however, will not go that far. But he wants more than the libertarian, more than the prevention of harm to others: he wants to prevent people's harming themselves. The position goes back to Aristotle's view that people who are not sufficiently rational to know what is good cannot rule themselves but should be governed by others. Aristotle was an aristocrat and a chauvinist. Among those incapable of self-government he included not only children but also women and some who "by nature" should be slaves. Today's paternalist is different. He still insists, however, that people often do not know what will harm them, or that emotionally they cannot accept what they know, or that they cannot control themselves. Legislation is therefore needed not only to outlaw dueling, for example, but also perhaps to require the wearing of seat belts in automobiles. Attitudes to gun legislation, to pornographic magazines, to drunkenness, drugs and gambling, likewise vary among libertarians, legal moralists and paternalists. Within this spectrum of viewpoints, where might a Christian ethic place us?

Some Preliminaries
Rather than jumping quickly to conclusions, I want to pause and sort through some of the ingredient concepts. With regard to morality two questions arise. First, the twin principles of justice and love require respect for the equal rights of all persons and a positive concern for their good. A conflict of duties may thus arise. If we are convinced that homosexual behavior or hallucinogenic drugs or drunkenness is harmful to a person physically, psychologically or morally, then we will want to prevent his doing such things to himself. This is a paternalist

direction. Should we legislate accordingly? Christian concern for justice will want to respect individual rights, even the right to be wrong and suffer the consequences. Which way then shall we go? Paternalist or libertarian?

Second, the matter is aggravated when we think back to the basis of moral obligation (chapter eight). Moral duty is neither autonomous nor self-imposed. Nor is it heteronomous, imposed by social expectations or by desirable consequences. Rather it is theonomous, God-given. This is what motivates the legal moralist, the conviction that God's law takes precedence over all private moralities and social mores. Yet God *covenanted* with Israel when he gave the law at Sinai, and Israel *agreed* to make God's moral law the law of their national life. A consensual morality was therefore involved. How then can we legislate morality in a pluralistic society that lacks moral consensus?

Questions also arise regarding the law. First, on what basis does the authority of the law rest? A utilitarian like Mill adopts the legal positivist position that laws are posed by society for utilitarian ends; hence the libertarian conclusion that laws must not restrict liberties except on consequentialist grounds, to prevent harm to others. The law then has no relation to any but a utilitarian kind of ethic. The natural law theory of Thomas Aquinas, on the other hand, sees human laws as an application of eternal moral law to the social order.

I am more inclined to a natural law philosophy. Biblically, as we have seen, government is ordained by God to maintain a just and peaceable society, and this is a moral concern. The mandate is not only for conflict-resolution nor only for utility's sake. It is rather for a moral good (justice) intended by God for human society. The New Testament setting of this emphasis is a non-Christian culture, a religiously and morally pluralistic society rather than a theocracy as in the Old Testament (Rom 13; 1 Pet 2). Even in such pluralistic settings, let us note, an ethical basis for legislation pertains.

The second question concerns the *extent* of law in comparison with morality. The social justice required of government in Romans 13 is not the totality of God's moral law. It is significantly less than was legislated in the Mosaic code, and less than legal moralism requires. On a New Testament basis in a pluralistic society, then, governmental authority seems not to extend to legislation on private moral conduct. Rather, it applies to maintaining public order and the equitable treatment of all parties. In his *Treatise on Law* Thomas Aquinas declared that divine moral law is for our eternal good, the natural law is for our earthly good, and the human laws derived from it are for the common good in society.

This brings us to the distinction between private and public morality on which the Wolfenden report depended. That distinction, we find, is not just a utilitarian one, but it rests also on natural law and on biblical grounds. The problem is to define the distinction with sufficient precision. One response to the Wolfenden report came from a distinguished jurist, Sir Patrick Devlin. More than individual liberties is at stake, he argued, for some private moral practices can be tremendously harmful to society. This is obviously the case with crimes committed and plots laid (as most are) in secret, but it would also be true of activities that erode the moral basis of a social order. Such a basis is established cumulatively over a long span of history; in England, Devlin claimed, it largely followed the Judeo-Christian ethic. Hence a moral practice like homosexuality, even in private between consenting adults, if it were to become sufficiently widespread and sufficiently accepted, would erode the family structure which is a major strength of the nation. The practice might then even be regarded as treasonous. Devlin plainly recognized a moral basis to the social order and the function of law in upholding that order. But *private* does not simply mean "out of sight." Nor does it mean matters left to private judgment. It is rather that which tends to harm neither social order and stability nor other individuals. Devlin's position, however, is still stated in utilitarian rather than the legal moralist terms of the Old Testament.

But just what is meant by *harm*? This, too, can be very ambiguous, and some jurists speak of "harm and offense." Does harm have to be actually *felt* by people, or is a tendency or potential sufficient? Harm is not just physical; it can be psychological or economic, too. And what about moral harm? Certainly in the case of children this must be included. But should "adult movies" be banned because of their potential for moral harm to adults? How far can we go?

Further questions arise about the value of liberty in relation to other moral and social values. In no social philosophy and in no society can liberty be entirely unlimited. It is not the one supreme value; if it were, nothing should limit it but everything else should serve it. Liberty, rather, is a corollary of human rights and is thus an ingredient of justice. But justice is more than the administration of individual liberties; it also requires an equitable distribution of the benefits and costs of society. And justice is paramount in biblical talk of a political society.

Liberty came to the fore in modern times with the rise of Western political ideals in the eighteenth century. It was further elevated by nineteenth-century romanticists and sometimes associated with a divine creativity within us. Nietzsche absolutized it in his will to power, a driving force that knows no moral bounds. Plainly a Christian view of liberty will avoid such extremes, taking a more modest view that keeps our liberties within moral constraints. Yet individual liberty remains of high value, and both Mill and Devlin are right that extreme caution is needed if it is to be legally limited.

A Proposal

Apparently we cannot both preserve individual liberties and legislate all the aspects of morality we might think we ought.

Here is a case of conflicting obligations in which rule-governed exceptions to moral rules (chapter six) are needed. Devlin provides for this by extending Mill's harm principle into four rules for preserving liberties while legislating in matters of morality.[4] The law should:

1. preserve the maximum individual freedom consonant with the integrity of the social order;
2. be slow to act, for other restraints are available;
3. respect privacy as far as possible;
4. legislate a minimal morality only.

To these we might add four further rules:

5. To be enforceable, a law must have widespread public support and represent a consensual morality.
6. A law must be equitably enforceable.
7. Legislation should not be changed with every changing moral mood, since this undermines respect for the law and public order.
8. A law should avoid harmful side effects (like invasion of privacy or blackmail).

These are all morally based rules to govern exceptions to the rule against restricting individual liberties.

Consider Devlin's four rules once again. The first asks a *just cause* for restricting freedom. The second regards legislation as a *last resort,* or at least one of the last options to consider rather than the first. The third rule stipulates *limiting the means* of enforcement. The fourth sets *limited ends* for morals legislation.

The same four concerns, let us note in passing, frequently appear in other ethical discussions—for instance, on war and revolution, on civil disobedience and criminal punishment. In the just war theory, for example, the one *just cause* for conflict is the need to resist violent aggression; war is to be a *last resort* after every possible negotiation and compromise has failed; it may employ only *limited means,* proportionate to the *limited end* of restoring a just peace for all involved, friend and foe alike.[5]

Such rules attempt to prevent abuses of power, just as do morals legislation in a pluralistic society.

To limit morals legislation by larger ethical considerations, however, does not mean that nothing further may be done. Legislation is only one recourse, and the most extreme. Other avenues for persuasion exist, and in many matters of private morality they are at least as effective. Licensing and taxing bodies exercise some control. Boycotts and protests can influence policy. The media can expose moral conditions, arouse public concern and pressure for change. Moral education in the home, the school and the church can shape moral attitudes. The prophetic role of the church in society through its preaching, teaching and publications influences morals. And the witness of solid moral character to a righteous way of life must never be underestimated. Legislation is one of God's means of moral governance, but only one.

The conclusions to which we are drawn are then severalfold:

1. Government's mandate in regard to legislating morality is limited to matters of public justice and the social order.

2. Legal moralism in a pluralistic society is both impractical and unjust.

3. Limits to legislative power are necessary in any society.

4. We should avail ourselves first (and consistently) of alternative means of persuasion and social action.

The kingdom of God is with us now only in a small way; it is yet to come in its fullness. Only then will the law of God become the law of every land with equal justice for all and with full social consent. Until then we are to be the salt of the earth, a pervasive influence for righteousness, both public and private.

12

Sex and Marriage

M any of the topics we have already considered arise again as we look at the ethics of sex and marriage. Prostitution, pornography and homosexual activity pose questions about the legislating of morals. Sexual discrimination, egalitarian marriage and the abortion debate focus the demands of justice and human rights. The cultural diversity of sexual mores and the so-called sexual revolution of the last two decades reintroduce ethical relativism and pose renewed questions about moral knowledge.

Current attitudes toward sex and marriage reveal a pervasive ethical egoism. In some cases *Playboy*'s hedonism is at work, limited only by a harm principle reminiscent of Mill. Using women as means of sexual enjoyment, it tends to depersonalize them and to evoke proper feminist outrage. In other cases sex has become narcissistic, marriage a means to individual fulfillment. Husband and wife alike, in an individualism that can breed distrust and become destructive, have become means to each other's ends. Egoism backfires because, as was argued earlier, we naturally need and desire something other than our own satisfaction. An adequate ethic of sex and marriage must recognize that phenomenon, just as it must also insist on the equal dignity and rights of both sexes.

The old, popular approach to sexual morality argued for extramarital abstinence in purely consequentialist terms, from the fears of conception, detection and infection. This triple deterrent may have been persuasive in another age, but not today. The pill has greatly reduced the first fear, changed social attitudes have reduced the second, and modern drugs the third. In any case, consequentialist arguments, like utilitarian stances in any age, have limited ethical significance. They allow, as we saw in chapter five, whatever good we want to maximize; but it is not at all clear that the new sexual freedom is the highest good in this area. They assume we can predict outcomes aright; but unforeseen and unwanted pregnancies still occur, and broken marriages increase. Meanwhile the problem of equal rights surfaces not only for broken relationships and the children of broken marriages, but also in women's ready access to abortion on demand.

Even such a quick overview of the sexual scene points up the need for an ethic that goes beyond egoist and consequentialist approaches. Sex for individualistic ends can be a manipulative, chauvinistic and destructive power play that ignores what justice and love might require.

In this, as in any area of moral responsibility, the Christian recognizes obligation to God. A sexual relationship is not confined to just two persons: it also involves God, the Creator and Lord of us all, who for his own good purposes made us the sexual beings we are. Christianity is not alone in asserting a religious dimension here. In the ancient world religious prostitution celebrated nature's fertility. At the other extreme, celibacy is still sometimes embraced as a religious calling. More pertinent to sex generally is the Old Testament rite of circumcision, adopted as a sign that God's covenant was with the children of Abraham for generation after generation. The genitals themselves were therefore to be a constant reminder that one's sexuality is God-given and that we are responsible in sex to God.

Sexual union and reproduction are part of God's creation, ordained from the beginning in the institution of marriage. Sex must not be taken out of this context and treated in a purely biological and psychological fashion, as often happens in contemporary society. Its ultimate meaning is not to be found in itself, in the act, the experience or even the social consequences. As with anything at all viewed theistically, its ultimate meaning is to be found in relation to God and his purposes.

In discussing moral knowledge (chapter seven) we suggested a pattern for moral reasoning that asks three questions:

1. What universal human action spheres are involved?
2. What essential purposes inhere in the nature of those activities as created by God?
3. How can these purposes best be pursued with justice and love?

Purposes Pertaining to the Sexual Sphere

What inherent moral indicators appear generically in human sexuality? What features of sex speak to its intended ends?[1] The history of Christian ethics is quite explicit in this regard: the psychology of sex indicates its unitive potential, and its biology indicates a reproductive potential. In both cases I stress "potential," for not every sex act is ipso facto unitive, bonding a couple in mutual love and commitment. Sex can also alienate and dominate a partner. And by nature not every sex act can be biologically reproductive. But a sexual relationship has so plain a reproductive potential that childless marriages without planning are the exception.

Sexual attraction marks the beginnings of a unitive potential, and we still speak of a single sex act as consummating that union. But the ongoing sexual relationship of a couple even more plainly has the capability of nourishing love, expressing tender concern, eliciting honesty and trust, and renewing commitment. It can bind a couple ever more closely and firmly together. The Song of Solomon delights in these realities. But sexual union is not just physical. In its full realization it involves entire lives—the emotions, goals and values, the economic resources and social contribution of two people. It therefore defies egoism and points the way to mutual responsibility and service.

The Bible speaks of raising a godly heritage, of transmitting the faith and the hope it promises to successive generations. It is the combination of reproductive and unitive potential which makes that possible, for a full expression of the unitive potential encompasses children with ideals and influences which they in their turn could pass on to others. We speak of the family as the basic unit of society, so that the stability and moral quality of society reflect that of the family unit. Appropriately so, for once again the unitive potential of sex can help nurture concern for others and a willingness to serve unselfishly in meeting the needs of broader segments of society.

Observe where these moral indicators lead. The combination of unitive and reproductive potential points to the wholistic relationship we know as heterosexual marriage, with a mutual love, honor and caring that are faithful and enduring. It rules out extramarital and premarital affairs as superficial and banal in comparison, a far cry from the fuller meanings of sex intended by the Creator. Nor does it mean that "anything goes" within marriage, for sexual enjoyment is not the ultimate consideration any more than hedonistic ends generally are in other human activities. These indicators help explain the tragedy and trauma associated with divorce. In all of this, biblical morality makes a great deal of sense.

Similarly this line of thought explains why Paul calls homosexual activity unnatural (Rom 1:26-28). He may have had in mind
some idea of a natural moral law as well as the Old Testament
law, for he is speaking of our sexual nature in a generic sense,
not of individual psychological differences (Lev 18:22; 20:13).
That homosexual tendencies may be deeply ingrained in some
individuals does not deny the inherent potential of human sexuality of which we have spoken, nor in God's creation does it deny
these potentialities moral import. Homosexual tendencies call
for our understanding and care, not for exceptions to or changes
in the moral law. Homosexual relationships outside of marriage
are still, by definition, fornication. And a homosexual marriage
would violate the intent of sex for a reproductive union to raise
a godly heritage.

This poses further questions about contraception and the
childless marriage. In the early church, objection was frequently
raised in one and the same breath to contraception, abortion
and infanticide. This may have been a response to pagan disre-
gard for the sacredness of human life generally as a gift from God,
for certainly Christians cannot regard having children as something to be decided purely on the basis of self-interest. It is part
of the stewardship of life and of the life-producing potential
with which God has gifted us. But the early objections may have
been due also to Stoic animalculist genetics, whereby the father's
seed was supposed to contain a complete miniature offspring,
body and soul entire. Such a view would pose equal problems
for contraception as for abortion and infanticide.

The natural reproductive potential of human sexuality does
not argue against responsible contraception, however, for by
nature not every sex act is intended to be reproductive. What it
rather indicates is, first, that only in a marital context is the sexual
relationship proper and, second, that the prima-facie expectation
is for the marriage to bear children. This potential for parenthood
must be responsibly exercised in the light of one's ability to

parent effectively. Too large a family in an overpopulated world would be irresponsible, as would be the selfish avoidance of having a family without regard for what God intends marriage to be. And in some cases the prima-facie expectation may be overridden by other moral responsibilities.

Applying the Principles of Justice and Love

What do justice and love require in regard to sex?

The word *love* is of course ambiguous, and all the more so on this topic. We must distinguish the three Greek words translated "love": *erōs,* which is sexual desire and attraction; *philia,* which is friendship love; and *agapē,* which is self-giving love.

Erōs is possible independent of *philia* and *agapē.* It can even create a romantic atmosphere. But by itself it is possessive and tends to be hedonistic; it is not a whole-person attachment, and its satisfactions do not last. But *philia* combined with *erōs* moves the relationship in a wholistic direction and makes possible a lasting and satisfying marriage. A spouse then is also a best friend, and a good marriage enjoys the reciprocal benefits of good friendship.[2] *Philia* brings qualities that enrich *erōs,* elevating it to more than a sensual and other than a possessive relationship.

Love as a moral principle, however, is *agapē.* Combined with *erōs* and *philia,* it leads beyond the confines of mutual benefit into a self-giving concern for others. *Agapē* transforms *erōs* from self-indulgence to tender care, and it changes marriage from a relationship focused on just itself into a powerful means for unselfish service to others.

This seems to be behind Paul's call for *mutual* submission as he addressed the relationships within a family (Eph 5:21). On his analogy, the wife's loving service can resemble that of the church for Christ, and the husband's that of Christ for his church. Unselfish, loving service, a two-way street within marriage, then finds widening outreach.

But love is not the only absolute moral principle. Justice is significant as well, and love *(agapē)* moves us to seek equal justice for all. What then has justice to say to sex and marriage? In the first place, it speaks against sexual abuse, taking advantage of others sexually against their will or better judgment. This applies to practices which the Bible addresses explicitly, like seduction (Ex 22:16), rape (Deut 22:28-29) and incest (Lev 18:6-18; Deut 22:30; 1 Cor 5:1-2), as well as to prostitution and pornography, which take commercial advantage of a person's moral weakness. Justice also speaks against sexual discrimination, for all persons have equal human rights, both male and female being in the image of God (Gen 1:26-28).

Since justice is the concern of government, legislation should exist to protect victims of sexual abuse, to punish violators and to correct sexual discrimination. But justice is also concerned about the rights of marriage partners. Even primitive societies have firmly embedded mores related to marriage and divorce. In modern societies the legalization of marriage is an extremely important social and economic protection, and divorce laws are intended to protect the rights of both the partners and their children when a union breaks apart. Jesus recognized the importance of this when he commented that Moses allowed divorce because of human hardness (Mt 19:3-8; Deut 24:1-4).

The claims of justice extend to the equal rights of both partners within a marriage. However their respective roles may vary from society to society and through social change, equal rights should invariably be a concern. The woman is not chattel to be used and discarded at will. Even slaves in Old Testament times were protected from that, as was the unloved wife in a polygamous marriage (Ex 21:7-11; Deut 21:10-17). The frequency of divorce today underscores the continued importance of legal safeguards. While not all details of marital justice can be enforced legally, the moral issue of justice is always present, and emphasis on women's rights is essential.

The key ethical question we are pursuing is how God's *purpose* in marriage may be advanced with *justice*. Family structures and authority patterns (like economic systems and political structures in their spheres) are *means* to that end, not fixities to be preserved for their own sake. The patriarchal and hierarchical arrangements of another era may not be so effective in an age when women have the same educational advantages and can have the same professional or business experience as men. To pour women into molds fashioned for a semiliterate and largely agrarian society, into roles that stifle the stewardship of their God-given gifts and opportunities, is neither loving nor just. Justice calls for equal rights in marriage, and modern marriage is having to adjust to this call. Yet the danger in the other extreme is great, the danger of individualists' ignoring the purpose of marriage as a nucleus of service to others.

In discussing sexual ethics, finally, we cannot ignore the single person who, from whatever cause, remains unmarried. Marriage as a union of loving service to others passes such persons by, along with marital sexuality that enriches both life and love. But the single person remains a sexual being, gifted by God for good. Our sexuality, as we have to remind ourselves in a sex-soaked culture, is expressed not just genitally. It also finds expression in friendships and in the mutual contributions that we can make socially. Our highest good is not found in sex or marriage, and both love and justice can operate to the full in other ways. Jesus was single, and he observed that some people choose to be single for the sake of his kingdom (Mt 19:10-12). The apostle Paul noted advantages to singleness, benefits which he had undoubtedly experienced himself (1 Cor 7:32-35). The basic point is clear: both marriage and singleness find their meaning and purpose outside themselves.

13

The Ethics of Virtue

*T*o this point we have concentrated on the ethics of human conduct, on principles and rules that should govern our actions. But there is more to morality than doing what is right and good. If I drive within the speed limit only because a police car is following me, I may be doing what is right, but I do it for prudential rather than ethical reasons. I may perhaps drive within the speed limit merely to annoy my companion and make him late for an important engagement. Then I would be doing what is right from a morally wrong motive. Again, I might keep the speed limit just because my car won't go any faster. Then I would be doing what is right unintentionally.

Motives and intentions as well as actions are morally significant. Even more than my actions, they reflect the kind of person I am, my inner disposition and character. To be peaceably disposed, a generous and patient person, is virtuous. But self-

centeredness, animosity and greed are vices. In this final chapter,
then, we turn our attention from the moral act to the moral
agent, from conduct to character, from rules to virtues, from
what we do outwardly to the kinds of persons we should be
inwardly.

What Is a Virtue?

The Bible places greater importance on moral virtue and character than it does on rules of conduct. The righteous man and
the pure in heart are eternally blessed, and the fruits of the
Holy Spirit described in Galatians 5 are all virtues. Until modern
times the history of ethics likewise gave at least as much weight
to the virtues as it did to actions. Plato extolled and examined
the classical virtues of wisdom, courage, temperance and justice,
to which Aquinas later added the religious virtues of faith,
hope and love. Aristotle examined other virtues too, and more
systematically, looking also at the development of moral character and at the weakness of will that undermines it. Biblical
and Greek influences together are the sources of our heritage
in this area.

What is a virtue? I referred just now to motives, intentions
and underlying dispositions. What these have in common, first,
is that they are all *inner* states rather than overt behaviors
and, second, that they are *affective* rather than purely cognitive
states. A virtue is a right inner disposition, and a disposition
is a tendency to act in certain ways. Disposition is more basic,
lasting and pervasive than the particular motive or intention
behind a certain action. It differs from a sudden impulse in
being a settled habit of mind, an internalized and often reflective
trait. Virtues are general character traits that provide inner
sanctions on our particular motives, intentions and outward
conduct.

Kant spoke of self-mastery, of the power to master our inclinations when they rebel against the moral law, of the moral

strength of a person's will in fulfilling his duty.[1] The language is that of his particular ethic of duty, but its significance is much broader: virtues are affective inner states, tendencies to action. A developed character makes behavior far more predictable than does the sudden impulse or passing inclination. It makes a person reliable, a responsible agent.

The crucible of moral decision demands not only moral principle and moral reasoning about what we should do, but it also requires the moral disposition to choose and do what is right. I am told that 67 per cent of young women and 80 per cent of young men have sexual relations by the age of nineteen. Is it that these young people are morally ignorant or that they have faulty moral reasoning? Or is it rather the result of impulsive or conformist dispositions and a commentary on moral character? Knowing what is right does not itself move or restrain us. Inner dispositions do.

Elements of Good Character

What are right dispositions, and how should we decide what they are? The question is complicated by cultural relativism when we consider, for instance, the virtue of "magnificence" which Aristotle extolled, or Benjamin Franklin's conception of thrift, or Nietzsche's call for a transvaluation of values. Dispositions commended in one culture or at one time in history do not always retain their status. Consider too the traits desirable to inner-city gangs and compare those with the values of affluent suburban adults. Yet in the ethics of virtue, as in previous considerations, diversity does not prove that *all* moral standards and virtues either are or should be completely relative.

The same is true of the apparent theory-dependency of virtues. The ethical egoist we considered earlier regards self-serving actions and rules as right, the "trait-egoist" adopts as virtuous those tendencies which are conducive to his own welfare, and the "trait-utilitarian" adopts those conducive to the maximum good of the most people.[2] In contrast, the "trait-deontologist" holds that a trait is virtuous in and of itself rather than because of its consequences. Kant, for example, valued rational self-mastery for its own sake: nothing, he said, is good without qualification other than a good will. Yet none of this theory-dependency proves that virtues are relative.

Plato tried to avoid trait-relativism by relating the virtues to the universal nature of persons. Wisdom is virtue of intellect, courage is the virtue of the spirited element in us, self-control is virtue in relation to the appetites, and justice is the harmonious unity of all these elements under the rule of reason.[3] Aristotle followed this precedent by identifying intellectual virtues that pertain to the rational soul and moral virtues that apply to irrational elements like desire.[4]

We, too, might well pursue this route, as we did with universal human action spheres. For the theist the question is what kind of disposition God wanted us to develop when he created us as he did. What is it to be a human person? What kind of moral character does this imply? This form of questioning pushes us further than an analysis of human personality as such, because God created us in his own image and likeness. Justice and love are central to God's moral character. If these are virtues that characterize God, so that he always acts out of justice and love, then they should characterize us too. The virtuous woman and the righteous man are alike just and loving with godlike charac-ter. They will tend to act toward others as God incarnate did— and as he would do in our place. Jesus Christ, the ideal man, becomes the model for human virtue.

These overall virtues of justice and love, then, should pervade those traits associated with specific aspects of human personality. Augustine, for example, reinterpreted Plato's four virtues.[5] Wisdom, he said, is love distinguishing what helps it toward God from what might hinder it; courage is love bearing every-thing readily for God's sake; self-control is love keeping itself entire and incorrupt for God; and justice is love serving God only and therefore ruling all else well. Virtue, then, is perfect love for God. Aquinas, on the other hand, treats the religious virtues of faith, hope and love separately as an addition to the four natural virtues.[6]

In both cases, however, the point is that the Christian virtue of love is something distinctive, something which the Greeks did not conceive of as a natural virtue. Plato talks of love as self-interested desire, *erōs*; Aristotle talks of friendship as in our mutual interest. But Christian love, like the love of God, is unselfish, even sacrificial in its compassion for others. And that affects every other virtue and the whole of a person's character.

When we ask, however, what virtues to seek beyond the fundamental ones of justice and love, we might well pursue the Greek method of looking for good traits that underlie various areas of conduct. Aristotle claimed that they lie between two extremes, the excess and deficiency of a personal characteristic. In the face of danger, for example, courage lies between the excesses of foolhardiness and the deficiencies of cowardice. In the use of our resources, generosity falls between extravagance and stinginess. In handling our appetites, self-control finds a mean between self-indulgence and complete disinterest. In relations to others, friendliness lies between being obsequious and being grouchy. The virtues are dispositions to act in a morally responsible way, the vices in an irresponsible way.

But look more closely at traits affecting our relation to others and ourselves. We might think of conscientiousness, yet conscientiousness alone is not enough. There have been conscientious Nazis, ruthlessly persistent in their anti-Semitic vendettas. Conscientiousness, perhaps more than other virtues, needs the larger characteristics of justice and love if it is to serve moral ends. We think also of generosity, and of an irenic and forgiving spirit. The apostle Paul listed joy, peace, patience, kindness, goodness, faithfulness, gentleness and self-control, as against vices like selfishness, jealousy, self-indulgence and a militant spirit (Gal 5:19-23). Such virtues are plainly dispositions in keeping with the overall virtues of justice and love.

Acquiring Virtuous Traits

What about character development and moral education? Aristotle saw virtues as habits of mind that can be cultivated. They do not arise naturally in the course of time, and they often run against our seemingly natural tendencies. Nor are they due merely to formal instruction. They require external controls initially, for discipline and regulation are conducive to good habits. Yet habits of mind are neither unconscious nor altogether involuntary. They develop as a result of deliberation about the choices we constantly make and the ends we desire. We are responsible agents in our own character development. The wicked may act *in* ignorance but not *out of* ignorance: they act rather out of bad character. The weak-willed do not act out of ignorance either; they act rather out of emotional distractions that they have never brought themselves to control. But the virtuous act out of good habits of mind internalized by repeated reflection and decision. As Kant put it centuries later, virtues are "considered, firm and continuously purified principles."[7]

I find Aristotle's account substantially correct. But it is challenged from two points of view. First, the eighteenth-century Enlightenment developed a far more rationalistic psychology in which a clear and distinct understanding has the power to overrule and subdue our passions and desires. Reason prevails over immediate self-interest so that we organize a civil society and agree to live harmoniously under the rule of laws. To this rule of reason David Hume articulately objected. Human actions, he insisted, spring from the passions and will rather than from reason itself.[8] Reason alone is inert and impotent, and its civil laws derive their authority not from their rationality but from our self-interested feelings. Augustine, in response to Cicero's Stoicism, takes a similar stand in Book 19 of *The City of God*. We are ruled not by reason alone but by what we love; in a civil society we are bound together not by the rule of reason but by agreement as to what we love. This, I suggest, is more akin to Aristotle's reflective choice than to the Enlightenment's prevailing reason. Aristotle, Hume and Augustine all insist that it is the will's orientation, not reason alone, that is morally decisive.

In the meantime, another objection arises, spinning off from the emphasis on inclination and desire. Sigmund Freud claims, for example, that human behavior is controlled by inner drives, and that "conscience" is merely the subconscious internalization of external controls. Character, then, is merely a set of inner sanctions for which we are in no way responsible. This is the determinist objection to freedom in character formation.

A major difficulty with the deterministic view arises when it is applied to itself. Determinism is not a view we can hold "responsibly," nor are we free to either accept or reject it. The determinist's acceptance of it is itself determined, so that he cannot meaningfully say that it is true independently of what he or we may think. We think what we are constrained to think, just as we have the inner traits we have—willy-nilly. But self-referentiality is not the only problem with determinism, for a further difficulty arises over the hasty generalization involved. That external regulation does affect character formation Aristotle himself affirmed. But that it accounts entirely for the totality of character formation he rightly denied. The determinist view is overgeneralized when it claims that all causes are of one sort. Aristotle saw the agency of the human will in its own choices as another kind, one that is inseparable from moral responsibility and moral character. The will can choose to initiate happenings and has the power to make a difference.

The role of the will may be seen in the way we resist temptation.[9] I am urged and drawn by my inner nature, even by elements in my present character, in some morally bad direction. The path of least resistance, the most natural thing for me to do, in fact, would be to yield. But sometimes another desire is present that resists the temptation. It takes an effort of will to choose aright—and resolute strength of will to fight it through. But in doing so, I strengthen the tendency to do what is right and thereby contribute to shaping my own character. Aristotle called this strength (as distinct from weakness) of will.

Approaches to moral education should be evaluated in this context. The psychologist Lawrence Kohlberg has charted six stages in cognitive moral development, culminating in an internalized habit of moral thinking, that may well prove helpful as a guide to character formation.[10] But character development, although cognitive, is *more* than a cognitive process; it also involves the strengthening of will and redirecting of desire. Augustine reminds us here again that virtue is the *love* of what is just and good. But how can this love be developed? How can we encourage a hunger and thirst for righteousness?

Here we have to move beyond Aristotle. Early discipline and a well-ordered environment may set an initial direction. Instruction may help to clarify ideals and even make them attractive. Parental models and peer models certainly contribute. Continued reflection and repeated choices will help us internalize. But Christianity, while it recognizes the role of all these, points us beyond them to the grace of God.

The gospel calls us to repentance and forgiveness. Repentance begins with a searching reflection on my actions and underlying habits of mind and culminates in a reversal of my attitudes—first toward God, and consequently toward myself and others. Forgiveness is a liberating thing, freeing me from the guilt that holds me back and creating a love for the God who forgives. Love brings hope, a hope that looks for help to the God I trust.

Love, said the apostle, is therefore the fruit that God's Spirit produces in us. This must be the capstone of any Christian ethic. Moral law can make us see our guilt and lead us to repentance and forgiveness. Biblical moral teaching and a Christian ethic can instruct us in righteousness. The fellowship of the church can model and encourage righteous living. But in the final analysis it is the grace of God that builds within us the virtues of godly character.

Notes

Chapter 2: Cultural Relativism

[1]William Graham Sumner, *Folkways* (1906), reprinted in *Ethical Relativism,* ed. John Ladd (Belmont, Calif.: Wadsworth, 1973), p. 23. Ladd's collection provides a convenient representation of material on this subject. For critical discussion see also Eliso Vivas, *The Moral Life and the Ethical Life* (Chicago: Univ. of Chicago Press, 1950), pt. 1; Abraham Edel and May Edel, *Anthropology and Ethics,* rev. ed. (New Brunswick, N.J.: Transaction Books, 1970); and Paul W. Taylor, "Four Types of Ethical Relativism," *Philosophical Review* 63(1954):500-516. See also Millard J. Erickson, *Relativism in Contemporary Christian Ethics* (Grand Rapids, Mich.: Baker Book House, 1974).

[2]Clyde Kluckhohn, "Ethical Relativity: Sic et Non," *Journal of Philosophy* 52 (1955):663-77.

[3]William Frankena, *Ethics,* 2d. ed. (Englewood Cliffs, N.J.: Prentice-Hall, 1973), p. 110.

[4]On this issue of freedom and determinism, see William Hasker, *Metaphysics,* Contours of Christian Philosophy (Downers Grove, Ill.: InterVarsity Press, 1983).

[5]H. Richard Niebuhr explores five ways in which Christians have related to culture in his *Christ and Culture* (New York: Harper Torchbooks, 1951).

[6]These philosophers will be discussed further. On Hobbes see chap. 4 and on Butler chap. 7.

Chapter 3: Emotivist Ethics

[1]See also chap. 7.

[2]See, for instance, A. J. Ayer, *Language, Truth and Logic,* 2d ed. (New York: Dover Books, 1946), chap. 6.

[3]Charles L. Stevenson, "The Emotive Meaning of Ethical Terms," *Mind* 46 (1937). For fuller development see his *Ethics and Language* (1944; reprint ed., New York: AMS Press, n.d.).

[4]See, for instance, Willard V. O. Quine's famous essay "Two Dogmas of Empiricism," in *From a Logical Point of View* (Cambridge, Mass.: Harvard Univ. Press, 1953), pp. 20-46. On the nonempirical influence in science, see Thomas S. Kuhn, *The Structure of Scientific Revolutions,* 2d ed. (Chicago: Chicago Univ. Press, 1970); and Michael Polanyi, *The Tacit Dimension* (Garden City, N.Y.: Doubleday, 1966). Simpler statements of the issue may be found in Nicholas Wolterstorff, *Reason within the Bounds of Religion* (Grand Rapids, Mich.: Eerdmans, 1976).

[5]This position is developed by ethical descriptivists like Philippa R. Foot. See her "Moral Beliefs," *Proceedings of the Aristotelian Society* 59 (1958-59).

Chapter 4: Ethical Egoism

[1]See Paul C. Vitz, *Psychology as Religion: The Cult of Self-Worship* (Grand Rapids, Mich.: Eerdmans, 1977) for a critique of such tendencies.

[2]See Ayn Rand, *The Virtue of Selfishness* (New York: New American Library, 1961) and her novels *Atlas Shrugged* and *The Fountainhead.* For representative discussions for and against egoism, see David P. Gauthier, ed., *Morality and Rational Self-Interest* (Englewood Cliffs, N.J.: Prentice-Hall, 1970).

[3]Joseph Butler, *Fifteen Sermons upon Human Nature* (1726), esp. sermon 11.

[4]C. D. Broad, "Egoism as a Theory of Human Motives," in *Ethics and the History of Philosophy* (London: Routledge and Kegan Paul, 1952).

[5]Thomas Hobbes, *Leviathan,* pt. 1, chap. 13.

Chapter 5: Utilitarianism

[1]Jeremy Bentham, *An Introduction to the Principles of Morality and Legislation* (1789); John Stuart Mill, *Utilitarianism* (1861) and *On Liberty* (1859); Amartya Sen and Bernard Williams, eds., *Utilitarianism and Beyond* (Cambridge: At the University Press, 1982).

[2]Frankena, *Ethics,* chap. 3.

[3]Perhaps the best discussion of contemporary utilitarianism is by J. J. C. Smart and B. Williams, *Utilitarianism: For and Against* (Cambridge: At the University Press, 1973). For a historical survey, see Anthony Quinton, *Utilitarian Ethics* (New York: St. Martin's Press, 1973).

Chapter 6: Toward a Christian Ethic

[1]William Paley, *Principles of Moral and Political Philosophy* (1785; reprint ed., Houston: St. Thomas, 1977).

[2]Mill, *Utilitarianism* (Indianapolis: Bobbs-Merrill, 1957), p. 22.

[3]On these two principles of justice and love, see Frankena, *Ethics,* chap. 3; and Lewis Smedes, *Mere Morality* (Grand Rapids, Mich.: Eerdmans, 1983), esp. chap. 2.

[4]See especially Joseph Fletcher, *Situation Ethics* (Philadelphia: Westminster Press, 1966).

[5]On this topic see Paul Ramsey, *War and the Christian Conscience* (Durham, N.C.: Duke Univ. Press, 1961); and Robert Clouse, ed., *War: Four Christian Views* (Downers Grove, Ill.: InterVarsity Press, 1981), chap. 3.

Chapter 7: Moral Knowledge

[1]For example, see the appendix to C. S. Lewis, *The Abolition of Man* (New York: Macmillan, 1947).

[2]This group embraces philosophers like Shaftesbury, Hutcheson, Adam Smith and Bishop Butler. See Elmer Sprague, "Moral Sense," in *The Encyclopedia of Philosophy,* vol. 5, ed. Paul Edwards (New York: Macmillan, 1967), pp. 385-87.

[3]Butler, *Fifteen Sermons,* sermons 2 and 3.

[4]William Frankena, "Moral Point of View Theories," in *Ethical Theory,* ed. Norman Bowie (Indianapolis: Hackett, 1983).

[5]See G. E. Moore, *Principia Ethica* (Cambridge: At the University Press, 1903).

[6]W. D. Ross, *The Right and the Good* (Oxford: Clarendon Press, 1930).

[7]Immanuel Kant, *Foundations of the Metaphysics of Morals* (1785), sec. 1.

[8]Alan Donagan adapts this second formulation as his basic principle in developing an essentially Judeo-Christian ethic, in *The Theory of Morality* (Chicago: Univ. of Chicago Press, 1977).

[9]For example, Cicero *De Legibus* 1. 5. 18-19, 22-23.

[10]John Locke, *Essays on the Law of Nature,* ed. W. von Leyden (London: Oxford Univ. Press, 1948).

[11]Aristotle *Nicomachean Ethics,* bk. 1.

[12]Aquinas *Treatise on Law,* Q.94. Art.2.

[13]See Alan Johnson, "Is There a Biblical Warrant for Natural-Law Theories?" *Journal of the Evangelical Theological Society* 25 (1982):185-89.

[14]See Jacques Ellul, *To Will and To Do* (Philadelphia: Pilgrim Press, 1969), *The Ethics of Freedom* (Grand Rapids: Mich.: Eerdmans, 1976), and *The Theological Foundations of Law* (Garden City, N.Y.: Doubleday, 1960).

[15]Helmut Thielicke, *Theological Ethics,* vol. 1 (Philadelphia: Fortress, 1966), chaps. 19-22; Dietrich Bonhoeffer, *Ethics* (New York: Macmillan, 1955), pt. 1,

chaps. 4-5, and pt. 3, chap. 3. See also Arthur F. Holmes, *Contours of a World View* (Grand Rapids, Mich.: Eerdmans, 1983), chap. 11.

[16]Ross, *The Right and the Good*, chap. 2.

[17]Compare Lewis Smedes's discussion of the "channeling" of human life in *Mere Morality*.

Chapter 8: The Basis of Obligation

[1]G. E. M. Anscombe, "Modern Moral Philosophy," *Philosophy* 33 (1958):1-19.

[2]Jean Paul Sartre, *Existentialism*, trans. B. Frechtman (New York: Philosophical Library, 1947), p. 20.

[3]Kant, *Foundations of the Metaphysic of Morals*, sec. 2.

[4]See Locke's *Second Treatise on Civil Government* (1689).

[5]This Searle essay initially appeared in *Philosophical Review* 73 (1964); it has been repeatedly anthologized since.

[6]John Rawls, *A Theory of Justice* (Cambridge, Mass.: Harvard Univ. Press, 1971); also "Two Concepts of Rules," *Philosophical Review* 64 (1955).

[7]R. M. Hare's best-known work is *The Language of Morals* (London: Oxford Univ. Press, 1964). But on the ultimate question see also his *Essays on the Moral Concepts* (Berkeley: Univ. of Calif. Press, 1972), pp. 20-21, and "Ethical Theory and Utilitarianism," in *Contemporary British Philosophy*, ed. H. D. Lewis (London: Allen & Unwin, 1976), p. 113.

[8]Anscombe, "Modern Moral Philosophy," p. 6.

[9]See Paul Helm, ed., *Divine Commands and Morality* (Oxford: Oxford Univ. Press, 1981); Gene H. Outka and John P. Reeder, eds., *Religion and Morality* (Garden City, N.Y.: Doubleday, Anchor Books, 1973); Philip Quinn, *Divine Commands and Moral Requirements* (Oxford: Clarendon Press, 1978).

[10]The term *theonomous* is borrowed from Paul Tillich, *The Protestant Era* (Chicago: Univ. of Chicago Press, 1960), pp. 56-57. I am indebted to Robert M. Adams for drawing attention to this.

Chapter 9: Human Rights

[1]Some of the key pieces on the concept of human rights have been collected in A. I. Melden, ed., *Human Rights* (Belmont, Calif.: Wadsworth, 1970). On its history see Leo Strauss, *Natural Rights and History* (Chicago: Univ. of Chicago Press, 1963).

[2]Jeremy Bentham, "Anarchical Fallacies," selections reprinted in *Human Rights*, ed. A. I. Melden, pp. 28-39.

[3]Mill, *Utilitarianism*, chap. 5.

[4]That some relationship exists between a natural law ethic and human rights is clear. Jacques Maritain develops this in *The Rights of Man and Natural Law*

(New York: Scribners, 1943).

Chapter 10: Criminal Punishment

[1]An excellent introduction is Jeffrie G. Murphy, ed., *Punishment and Rehabilitation* (Belmont, Calif.: Wadsworth, 1973).

[2]Barbara Wootton, *Crime and the Criminal Law* (London: Stevens and Sons, 1963).

[3]See C. S. Lewis, "The Humanitarian Theory of Punishment," in *God in the Dock* (Grand Rapids, Mich.: Eerdmans, 1970), pp. 287-300; and Herbert Morris, "Persons and Punishment," in A. I. Melden, ed., *Human Rights* (Belmont, Calif.: Wadsworth, 1970), pp. 111-34.

[4]For further developments regarding this kind of approach, see A. C. Ewing, *The Morality of Punishment* (London: Kegan Paul, 1929); Sir Walter Moberly, *The Ethics of Punishment* (Garden City, N.Y.: Doubleday, Anchor Books, 1968).

Chapter 11: Can We Legislate Morality?

[1]Jonathan Blanchard in an Oberlin College speech in 1839. The statement is inscribed on a plaque dedicated to him in Blanchard Hall at Wheaton College, Illinois, of which he was the founding president.

[2]Some of the key essays on both the general topic and the Wolfenden report appear in Richard Wasserstroms, *Morality and the Law* (Belmont, Calif.: Wadsworth, 1971).

[3]See Mill, *On Liberty* (Indianapolis: Bobbs-Merrill, 1956), esp. chap. 1.

[4]See Patrick Devlin, *The Enforcement of Morals* (London: Oxford Univ. Press, 1965). See also J. N. D. Anderson, *Morality, Law and Grace* (Downers Grove, Ill.: InterVarsity Press, 1972); H. L. A. Hart, *Law, Liberty and Morality* (London: Oxford Univ. Press, 1963); Basil Mitchell, *Law, Morality and Religion in a Secular Society* (London: Oxford Univ. Press, 1967).

[5]See chapter 3 in *War: Four Christian Views,* ed. Robert G. Clouse (Downers Grove, Ill.: InterVarsity Press, 1981).

Chapter 12: Sex and Marriage

[1]For further implications of this approach, see Paul Ramsey, *Fabricated Man* (New Haven, Conn.: Yale Univ. Press, 1970).

[2]The classic discussion of friendship as a reciprocal benefit is in Aristotle's *Nicomachean Ethics,* bks. 8 and 10. The agapistic virtue of self-giving and possibly unrequited love is missing from that account; it seems to have been largely a biblical contribution to Western ethics. Hence the distinctiveness of Christian ideals of sex and marriage.

Chapter 13: The Ethics of Virtue

[1] Immanuel Kant, "The Doctrine of Virtue," pt. 2 of *The Metaphysic of Morals* (Philadelphia: Univ. of Pennsylvania Press, 1964).

[2] I borrow the terminology from William Frankena's *Ethics,* pp. 63-65.

[3] See Plato *Republic,* bk. 4.

[4] His discussion of virtue occupies books 2 to 7 of the *Nicomachean Ethics.* Alasdair MacIntyre argues with Aristotle that a human life is a whole, a unity whose character provides the virtues with an inner *telos,* or ideal end. The modern mind has fragmented life into an array of disparate roles without any unifying telos, thereby relativizing the virtues. See *After Virtue* (Notre Dame, Ind.: Univ. of Notre Dame Press, 1981).

[5] Augustine *On the Morals of the Catholic Church,* 15.

[6] This practice is followed by the Catholic philosopher Peter Geach in his recent book *The Virtues* (Cambridge: At the University Press, 1977).

[7] Kant, *Doctrine of Virtue,* p. 42.

[8] David Hume, *A Treatise on Human Nature,* bk. 3, pt. 1.

[9] Charles A. Campbell develops this argument in chapter 2 of *In Defense of Free Will,* Muirhead Library of Philosophy (Atlantic Highlands, N.J.: Humanities Press, 1967). Compare Paul's account in Romans 7:15—8:6.

[10] On this and the general topic of moral education, see Nicholas Wolterstorff, *Educating for Responsible Action* (Grand Rapids, Mich.: Eerdmans, 1980).

Further Reading

For works on specific topics, see items referred to in the notes of pertinent chapters.

General Introductions

William Frankena. *Ethics,* 2nd ed. Englewood Cliffs, N.J.: Prentice-Hall, 1973. A highly competent and helpful treatment by one of the most influential ethicists of the last half-century.

Richard Purtill. *Thinking About Ethics.* Englewood Cliffs, N.J.: Prentice-Hall, 1976. The most readable for beginners, it is carefully argued and treats both ethical theory and selected areas of applied ethics.

Paul W. Taylor. *Principles of Ethics: An Introduction.* Belmont, Calif.: Wadsworth, 1975. A somewhat fuller treatment with high philosophical quality.

Anthologies

These are typical course texts containing primary source selections, historical and contemporary, on major positions and problems in ethical theory.

Robert E. Dewey and Robert H. Hurlburt III, eds. *An Introduction to Ethics.* New York: Macmillan, 1977.

William K. Frankena and John T. Granrose, eds. *Introductory Readings in Ethics.* Englewood Cliffs, N.J.: Prentice-Hall, 1974.

Paul W. Taylor, ed. *Problems of Moral Philosophy.* 3d ed. Belmont, Calif.: Wadsworth, 1978.

History of Ethics

W. D. Hudson. *A Century of Moral Philosophy*. New York: St. Martin's Press, 1980. An insightful and up-to-date discussion of twentieth-century developments.

Alasdair MacIntyre. *After Virtue*. Notre Dame, Ind.: University of Notre Dame Press, 1981. A highly provocative study of the tension between two traditions in Western ethics, one that begins with Aristotle, the other leading to Nietzsche.

Paul Ramsey. *Nine Modern Moralists*. Englewood Cliffs, N.J.: Prentice-Hall, 1962. Valuable critical studies of some key figures by an influential Christian ethicist.

Henry Sidgwick. *Outlines of the History of Ethics*. New York: St. Martin's Press, 1967. A classical treatment up to about 1900.

Geoffrey J. Warnock. *Contemporary Moral Philosophy*. New York: St. Martin's Press, 1967. Surveys Anglo-American ethical theory since 1900.

Christian Ethics

Norman B. Geisler. *Ethics: Alternatives and Issues*. Grand Rapids, Mich.: Zondervan, 1971. A textbook approach arguing its own definite conclusions on both theoretical and applied topics.

James Gustafson. *Protestant and Roman Catholic Ethics*. Chicago, Ill.: University of Chicago Press, 1978. Explores the effect of varied theological beliefs on ethical thinking.

Edward R. Long. *A Survey of Christian Ethics*. New York: Oxford University Press, 1967. A comprehensive exposition of different types of theological ethics.

Lewis B. Smedes. *Mere Morality*. Grand Rapids, Mich.: Eerdmans, 1983. Written for the layperson yet informed by thorough scholarship, an approach to the moral law via justice and love. Extremely helpful.

Helmut Thielicke. *Theological Ethics*. 3 vols. Grand Rapids, Mich.: Eerdmans, 1966-69. A comprehensive treatment by a respected German theologian of the theological foundation of Christian ethics and its application to politics and sex.